THE MOST HATED MAN
IN THE WORLD

THE MOST HATED MAN IN THE WORLD

Andreas Stavrinides

Copyright © 2019 Andreas Stavrinides

The moral right of the author has been asserted.

Apart from any fair dealing for the purposes of research or private study, or criticism or review, as permitted under the Copyright, Designs and Patents Act 1988, this publication may only be reproduced, stored or transmitted, in any form or by any means, with the prior permission in writing of the publishers, or in the case of reprographic reproduction in accordance with the terms of licences issued by the Copyright Licensing Agency. Enquiries concerning reproduction outside those terms should be sent to the publishers.

Matador
9 Priory Business Park,
Wistow Road, Kibworth Beauchamp,
Leicestershire. LE8 0RX
Tel: 0116 279 2299
Email: books@troubador.co.uk
Web: www.troubador.co.uk/matador
Twitter: @matadorbooks

ISBN 978 1789016 895

British Library Cataloguing in Publication Data.
A catalogue record for this book is available from the British Library.

Printed on FSC accredited paper
Printed and bound in Great Britain by 4edge Limited
Typeset in 12pt Adobe Jenson Pro by Troubador Publishing Ltd, Leicester, UK

Matador is an imprint of Troubador Publishing Ltd

To my mother and father.
For everything.

Contents

Part I
ANATHEMA   1

Only the Wind	3
so stupid and so small	8
if it weren't for you	10
Gift of Water	11
the lie and the truth	12
what makes us special	13
The Spark	14
Two Poets	15
questions for the mountain	16
Death in the Garden	17
First Foul Deeds	18
Moments Before	19
It Lies Serene	21
For God's Sake	22
I Come, I Come. Why Dost Thou Call for Me?	23
Frothing Gulliver	24
Waiting for the Man	26
Bonfire Night	27

Said A Spark To His Brother	29
Just Something I Threw Together…	30
What We Don't Discuss	32
For the Birds	35
Stand Tall	37
Love Poem	38
Little Man	39
Cat's Stare	41
Femur Propping Up a Fence	42
Man of Love	44
Confession	45
Fox	46
Erdogan the Fool	48
Two Men	54
Cogito Ergo Sum	55
Time Plots Against You	56
What I Should Have Said	57
When I Think of Giving Up	59
This	60
justice for the primate	62
Cold Universe	64
Such Sustaining Glimpses	65
Good Question	68
This Paradise They Dream Of	69
Peccadilloes	70
A Moment Ago	72
In the Garden with You	73
The Life That Matters	74

S.M.	75
Of Paradise	77
A World Unblinking	78
Fire in My Lungs	79
What Is Poetry?	80
What They Cannot Imagine	81
The Question They Hate	83
Here Be Monsters	84
Lucky	86
If You Can Believe This	89
there are good days	91
Plagued	93
Slipstream	95
Forged of Steel	97
Teeth for Your Heels	98
my country right or wrong	99
Dark. Naked.	100
What We Truly Are	103
Flame	105
Signifying Nothing	106

Part II
LET MY PEOPLE GO   107

Part III
THE MOST HATED MAN IN THE WORLD   203

Blame	205
a place to go mad in	206
Daddy	207
The Thief, Laughing	208
The Process That I Am	209
A Revelation	210
Foundation of a Civilisation	211
Just the Facts	212
Why Things Are Shit	214
Divine the Right	215
Putin's Mother	216
My Country Right or Wrong	217
Love Poem	218
eggs in moonshine	219
Fear	220
The End of War	221
The Rose Centre 18.10.17	222
The Naming of the Animals	223
Time-Honoured Tactic	225
Hide and Seek	228
Ad Hoc Architects	231
A Few Thoughts on the Death of Anne Boleyn	233
Things We Say	235
prodigal	238

Cup of Poison	239
Always	242
The Glory of the World	244
fair to the clerics	246
secret self	247
Older	248
The Great Flood	250
In the Dark	251
holy words	252
unholy word	253
wanna set the world on fire	255
In Spades	256
jesuitical	258
The Human Duty	259
On Their Way	261
Everybody Wins	263
Love After the Fact	265
mirror mirror	267
Having It All	269
all we have left	270
The Knife Lies in Wait	271
In the Beginning	273
Drowning	276
The One Thing Heaven Can't Abide	277
Adventure with Foof	283
The Limpet	286
Frustration	287
blackbird stealing	288

the wren	289
Party's Over	290
My Own Nature	292
Fixed	293
Cetacean Creed	294
Too Dark	296
Going up the Line	297
Still Waters	299
The Most Hated Man in the World	301
The Feast of Reason	302
A Gentle Rally	303
When Slaves Met Free Men	304
Joshua Ben Joseph	305
Termites	308
The Diamond	309
What's the Point?	310
if they promise you paradise	314
specimen of vanity	315
Children of a Lesser God	316
Come, Exterminating Angel	319
If Only You'd Run	321
Butcher's Hook	322
String Theory	323
Stand Aside, Brutus! It's My Turn Now	325
Before You Give Power	329
In the Ranks of the Free Men	330

PART I

ANATHEMA

Only the Wind

You are brought to a
road.
On either side sheer
walls disappear into
the sky.
You are thrust, alone,
confused, down the
on-ramp.
"Why am I here?" you
ask.
"Where am I going?"
You get no answer.

There's no way back so
you stagger forward.
Others on the road
Stare about
bemused. You travel
with them. Some drift to
other groups, some stay with
you all the way. Some you
grow to love.

After just a few steps you
see body parts. A child
falls to the ground in front of
you, blood in her eyes,
mouth frothing. She convulses
and dies.

From somewhere far above
you think you catch the
sound of sniggering. But
perhaps it's only the wind.

Then someone steps on a mine;
Blown to smithereens as you watch.
You stare in horror
at the ground, but have no choice.
You must continue.

Soon you learn mine fields
litter the road, sometimes marked,
mostly not. Each step could
be your last.

Now and then a sign appears with
name and rough distance and you
all fall silent.

These unfortunates are borne on stretchers
and must continue forward, always
onward, with those who carry them.

Some march naked, the skin of
some stretched wire thin over
ribs. Some force the weak
to carry them on their backs
while they gorge and yawn, and no matter
how huge they grow, those who stagger
beneath them, the 'work-shy', the 'shiftless',
plod on.

As time passes you learn to laugh when
you can, make vows of love and
friendship, to forget what lies
ahead.

But always, always you are on the road.

And at those times, those times of music
and wine, marriage and tenderness;
when the road has its beauties and
compensations; the primrose bank,
a dance of dragonflies on a lily;
when your sure destination is a mythical place;
even then that insolent cackle,
that sniggering in the heights catches your ear.

And you wonder if such treasures
as you have been
granted are true consolations
or taunts to be snatched from you.

And you limp on regardless
as you must
as one-by-one those at your
side fall away.

Finally you are alone.

Somehow shells exploding
about your head have missed you,
tumours grew inside other bodies,
your heart kept on beating.

You staggered through the entire
war-zone-turkey-shoot
and at the far end,
as you near the end,
bent, haggard, you wheeze as you plunge
forward, grateful the road at last is turning to
dust.

And sprawled on the ground,
clutching your chest,
remembering those who fell before,
you could swear you catch the sound,
far distant, of a snigger.

so stupid
and so small

it's funny to think of all those people
in the world who if we'd only met them
would be lovers, friends, maybe enemies,
yet our eyes will never take in even one per
cent let alone meet them. they live
in the same world but may as well
have been citizens of pompeii. their lives
and ours remain unaffected by each other.

it is odd that someone we will love or have
loved has existed or exists in another place,
unknown to us, having who knows what
experiences? it is a mystery to me, the
mystery of otherness. they laugh and
cry and we carry on oblivious, yet one
day they may matter more to us than
anything else.

or maybe our soldiers killed someone who,
one day, would have been your wife or
husband, who might have saved your life
or the life of your child, and instead you never
knew they were even in the world.

we like to believe in 'the one', in destiny,
but truth is otherwise. we let people
starve or live in squalor who we'd
love just as much as anyone we've
ever loved. we are so stupid and so small.

"if it weren't for you
I'd have left hours ago!"
now she's only a memory
and he's always on time,
to his bitter sorrow.

Gift of Water

A wasp on the side of our bird bath drinks.
I watch it gulping down yet the water margin
Remains the same. I rescue one that is cast
Adrift, legs scrabbling as it floats leaf-like.
And I take great pleasure that this gift of
Water, given to the small creatures of our
Garden, helps life, even saves life in
The heat of the late August sun. Later I notice
That the wasps are coming from a nest
In the eaves of our house and I know
I will have to kill them.

when the lie
and the truth
stand side
by side the
lie reaches
for its gun
and the truth
must hide.

what makes us special,
more than chimps or apes?
we're so clever. it's not
souls that attract the beady
eyes of god but brains,
without which we're just
another monkey on the plains.

The Spark

Greeks in a beach car park below
Argue with Greek passion. A long
Haired, grey-haired man with a paunch
Gestures at a car. The group around
Him cluster in. A ba ba babble of fury
Over who knows what? A scratch?
I look down with Olympian disdain,
But anger is a flame and I feel the
Spark. Almost unconsciously I search
For a side to take, a side to blame.

Two Poets

Kavvadias staring out to sea at Argostoli,
Laskaratos, hat in hand, back to the great
Foe who stole from Lixouri what was rightfully
Theirs. Everywhere should be like this!
A statue at the entrance to honour the
Great poets. Except, a refinement – the
Statues of all the composers, painters,
Directors and other artists grovelling
At their feet. Where they belong.

questions for the mountain

the man questioned
the mountain. the people
of the mountain looked
down and smiled.
the man insulted
the mountain. the people
of the mountain held
their sides
and laughed.

Death in the Garden

Death came to our garden last night.
He stopped twenty feet from where
We slept and waited, hidden amongst
The green and living things of our border.
At first light, while we lay oblivious he
Got to work, that psychopath who commands
The fate of us all. Later I flung the curtains
Wide on the sun. Signs of our visitor's efforts
Littered the lawn and I went out for a closer
Look finding the discarded head of a pigeon,
Berry still in its beak as if to pay the ferryman,
Eye gazing up at me. And in my horror
I felt the ancient gratitude. That the great enemy
Of each of us had left our garden satisfied
With another life, and left us alone
For now.

First foul deeds
Then fine words.
A veneer of jam
On stinking turds.

Moments Before

Moments before he'd taken a photo,
Captured the kiss blowing towards him
Through hot Greek air. Now he
Can't bear to look at it, though it's his
Most precious possession.

Moments before she'd plunged into the sea,
That same sea where so many summers
They'd made memories. The kids had
Paddled here close to the spot where
Face down her heart exploded.

"Sorry I wasn't myself yesterday," said our rep.
"They'd been customers of mine for years,
Always holding hands." She sat, waiting for
Our flight to land, on the edge of the carousel,
Face wet, preparing her smile.

The old man in hell in paradise, sits at the bar,
Calling his children: "Dad! Are you having a lovely
Time?" How to say the words?

All around laughter in this death banished idyll.
Children chase each other, friends sip
Cocktails or lounge with paperbacks
While he packs her bags full of the things
That signify joy. In the evening he
Sits in a corner of the dining room
Alone, eating cardboard ice-cream.

When he's gone our waitress says:
"That's the man whose wife…"
She nods towards the beach
Through the window and mumbles some
Things I don't quite catch, and turns away
Eyes streaming. Sara goes to her and
Gives her a hug and I imagine myself in
The old man's shoes and I want to do
Something to alleviate his pain. But I am
Powerless. And though I feel sad I know
Tomorrow I will enjoy myself, and try not
To think of him too much,
As I wait my turn.

It lies serene as
Your conscience.
Light scarcely penetrates
The surface. I can't see
The other side. Indignant
I search for the biggest brick
I can find and hurl it
With all my rage,
Waiting for the splash
And the look on your face.

For God's Sake

Was it determined from the first moment
That I would write these words? That I
Would begin with the word "do" in my notebook
Then scribble it out? Not that this is any
Culmination, don't mistake me. But each
Movement of each atom, each fraction of
Spacetime, followed precisely the laws of
Physics and chemistry. Always, everywhere.
So did biology create free will or was it
The gift of the human mind? It's merely
Chemistry and physics fused with
No property that does not derive.
Do we mistake complexity for
Freedom? If there is none, the man
Who offends God cannot do otherwise,
And spite punishes him for what he
Must do, for what he is made to do by
The punisher. And the man who pleases;
What reward does he deserve?
But it's bleaker still. Hitler, Stalin, the
Killer of children, each act a dance
On the string that reaches back to the
Fingers of its author. I want to believe
In free will. Not for my sake, but for God's.

I Come, I Come.
Why Dost Thou Call for Me?

"How many brothers do I have?"
A new milestone but she manages
A smile listing them: "Three, darling,
Peter, Loulis, and Andreas."
He throws back his head and uncurls
A finger, wagging it slightly. "Andreas!
I remembered Peter and Loulis
But I couldn't think of Andreas!"
He's gripping the edge now with resolve,
As Death prises him off, a finger at a time,
And gives the lie to the tale we tell
Ourselves. Love lasts forever they say,
A solace of sorts in the face of unbearable
Loss. But it won't even last till the end
Of his days. Perhaps we do need
Supporting walls within our minds
To prevent collapse. But instead of
Fantasy I choose truth to help me
Bear the load, which does not crumble
When acquainted with itself. Back then
To Cyprus and to Citium, an apt return.

Frothing Gulliver

Think you're safe?
A young couple starting out in Berlin,
1912, families respectable, educated,
Liked by neighbours. Could they conceive
Two wars would shatter their world?
What would they say if you told them
They, and their children and grandchildren
Would die breaking nails on the walls of some
Dark bunker, choked on pesticide amid
The naked shameless bodies of strangers,
Skin stretched to lampshades, teeth
Extracted for gold?
"But such a thing can happen only once
In history. A coming together of unique
Conditions, not the least of which was
No one conceived it could happen."
Does knowing what men can do
Make them less capable?
It's the same nature seething in
The hearts of all your neighbours.

Of you. And me. War happens every day,
Rape happens every day, murder is
Quotidian for Man. Since Cain how many days
Do you think have passed when not one
Human life was lost at the hands of another?
Imagine now a grand enterprise by all the leaders
Of our world. A day, a single solitary day, without
A murder anywhere. How long to plan?
How to get the gangs and psychopaths on
Board, and those thousands of flashes of rage
Held over till tomorrow, the hatred,
Prejudice and cruelty caging itself for
One rotation of this chunk of rock. Divide by
Twenty-four and I say the task is still too great.
What keeps us safe is not that we're better
Than before or others now in different places.
It's simply this, the checks and balances,
Laws and constitutions, those fragile strings we
Wrap around frothing Gulliver which strain and
Groan and might snap at any moment.

Waiting for the Man

I wait for the man they tell me is my enemy.
"You must kill him!" they say.
The earth is warm beneath my belly.
A grasshopper climbs a blade of grass.
A blackbird sings.
Gently I blow on the grasshopper.
He sways and disappears.
My breath, my life, enfolding this small creature,
A gift. I think of the widow's mite, and
Wonder who's coming, and
A breeze gently blows across
My face.

Bonfire Night

The light has faded in the light,
So too the dark, which seems
To have whitened. And the still
Animated figures fixed in glee,
Sparklers whirling, or peering
Upwards at the now pastel colours
Exploding overhead. I want to say
You should move this! I want to say
You've ruined it! But instead I sound
Impressed: "You took this? They're
Yours? How old were they?" I was
Once like them, a bang, a flash
Of colour, a hint of danger and I
Was entranced. Those autumn
Nights, so vivid and alive. But
The magic goes from magic.
We learn the tricks. I remember
As if yesterday Susan passing me
Through the library door, glancing
Back. Her smile. Her eyes.

That was all it took to plant a barb
So deep that even now, decades
After, the hook cannot be disgorged.
Not a day goes by when I don't
Think of that face, hidden
In the darkness of my mind.
Protected from the light.

Said a spark to his brother,
"You're not of the fire."
The other made no reply
But caught in the kindling
And proved him a liar.

Just Something I Threw Together…

Two eyeballs lying in a bowl
Staring at nothing in Siamese
Blue. A heap of skin flopped fat
Inside out, nerves and corpuscles
Scream. Hair, long and blonde,
Draped on a cutting board beside
A small shag pile in a cup, wispy,
Wiry. Fat maggot tongue lolling
Over its companion coil of pink-red
Steaming tube. Nails and nostrils,
Membranes and sphincters,
Teeth arranged in a fractured smile.
The levers, brittle as polite loathing,
The pulleys, a scarlet mound of string and
Gristle. Lips kiss ears in a jar, and
A broth of blood languishes in a pan
Ready to boil. In the sink under
Running water, bowel, brain, kidneys,
Liver. And poking from beneath – an aorta,
Like a snorkel for the heart.

"I'm going to be sick!" I say, covering my mouth.
"What's it all for?"

"SOMETHING SPECIAL," says God
And with a ta-da flash of smoke
A woman steps forward, sublime,
Poised. I stare mesmerised.

"IT'S NOT THE INGREDIENTS,"
God winks.
"IT'S THE CHEF."

What We Don't Discuss

It's strange such an honest woman
Who would shrivel inside if she told a lie,
Who hates even 'white lies', should display
Such blithe disregard for truth.
We stray into the no man's land of religion.
In the UAE a woman who claimed she
Was raped is charged with extra-marital sex.
Only religion I say could distort reason
To such an extent. "The difference is
Christianity and Judaism learned to ignore
Large parts of their holy books, while
Islam hasn't. That's why they don't
Stone adulterers any more."
"It's because of Jesus," says my mother.
How could someone who has followed
This religion her entire life, steeped
In the Bible and Christian writings, miss
Such a basic point? "But Jesus is the same
God!" I put her own belief to her.
"The only reason they were stoning
People in the first place was that the very
Same God who now says only the sinless

Should cast stones was the one who commanded
Adulterers be stoned."
"I'm not discussing it with you!"
Always the same with religion. Don't think,
Don't think. And this my more rational parent.
Clearly something matters more than truth,
But what can it be? Who when a viper
Bites hugs it closer to their chest?
I imagine her following the logic
Of the contradiction into other questions
Until the brittle bone fragments and crumbles
To dust. What would it mean to her life?
She's just about holding it together with
Dad's Alzheimer's and health problems
Of her own, her weekly prayer
Group, close vital friends, her belief the whole
Framework of her life. The lease
Is nearly done. Who would contemplate
Rebuilding, right from the foundations
At this late date? Who's being more
Practical and who the ideologue? And yet,
Is a lie really the best way to face reality?
So many lies we tell, but what hope
If we deceive ourselves? She also tells me:
"You're not to question Alexia's faith."
Obviously not confident she can

Withstand my wiles. And again,
What of the truth?
These are people I love.
I don't want to tempt them to harm.
I want to release them, to allow them to think.
And if it can be justified as a crutch why insist
On Christianity in particular?
"Because the others are all lies."
And they'd be only too pleased to follow me down
Any avenue of questioning reason leads to prove
their point.

For the Birds

You see that hen on its nest,
Ready to die for possibility?
It's not exactly an act of faith,
She hasn't even such low
Intelligence. What then?
Hope? What can she hope for?
The same for them as for herself.
Pecking for grain and grubs,
Feeling the beetles' hard shells
And pin-stiff legs scratch the inside
Of her throat. Hopping, flapping,
Loveless, unloved, unknown.
Hunger, thirst, cold, heat.
Slumped stoic in the rain.
Anxious by default, punctuated
With terror. And death.
Undoctored, alone, perhaps
Teeth or talon savaging her flesh.
That which was joined together
Torn asunder, swallowed.
Endless digestive musical chairs.

In bits in acid, and then Death's
Final transfigurative sneer.
Patiently she sits there and I hope
For their sake those eggs will
Never hatch.

Stand Tall

Stand tall, they said,
With your head held
High. Don't keep
Looking at your feet!
And so I stepped out
Proud among the people.
And soon trod in a turd
In the street, stinking,
Sticky, and wet.

Love Poem

"Why do you want kisses?
It's so tiresome."
I stand by the front door.
"That's nice. Just what every
Husband wants to hear."
She flops over from the kitchen
In her pyjamas laughing and
I smother her face.
"I'll write a poem about it.
A love poem."

Little Man

You speak, Mr Assad, of terrorists in Aleppo and I wonder
If a man or woman who seeks to assert their own political
Destiny, a voice, freedom from state control, who wants a say
In the running of their country, and who wields its power, is
What you mean when you wield this word? Is this a man you'd
Torture and kill, whose kids you'd send your henchmen to butcher?
Are people like that to be barrel bombed and gassed?
If that's your definition, encompassing everyone I know
And have loved or admired then I too am a proud terrorist.
Let me be a terrorist for daring to ask: "Where's your legitimacy,
Little man? Who put you in charge?" Did God come to you
In a dream? Perhaps it's ok to want these things as long as you
Don't insist or aren't willing to fight. Like Oliver Twist's gruel,
Dished out as benevolence, "we keep you alive and you're so ungrateful!"

Is that it? And your use of this word 'terrorist', it justifies
Anything these days. A magic bullet people like you conjure with
When someone resists. The first of many. "I'll steal your freedom,
I know best, and if you think otherwise or stir up trouble by uttering
Your own opinions see what happens." There must have been
Something in your mother's water to make you so special.
You know you're a usurper, but do you even care? And is it
Terrorism if a slave plunges a knife through his master's
Throat as payment for his stolen life? It's what you deserve.
I'd do it myself if I could.

A mouse beneath a cat's stare
Is not free. "Ah, but I won't be a cat,"
Says the cat. "I give you my word."

Femur Propping Up a Fence

In the garden where police search, a femur
Propping up a fence, put to good use
Now it's no longer needed by its first owner.
Like all things, held in being by the will
Of the Creator, so clever men insist. He keeps it
There, doing its practical task for the practical
Man who valued its load-bearing properties
Too much to be rid of it, though it has a voice
That screams and implores. Part of a woman
Holding up a fence. Grotesque, is it?
Are we alone in thinking so? This thing that
Skipped and ran, hopscotched and hid,
Held close perhaps someone special.
God honours the acts of this man, holds them
In being, not just the killing, dismembering, but
"Now you are part of a fence, who were a person."
He keeps it there, hour after hour, year after year,
Adopting the act as His own. So easy to move it.
The man would think a fox had taken it away – He
Could even plant the thought. So why
Leave it there? Except this is the logic of
Evil in the world. Unravel a thread and the

Tapestry of depravity goes with it. Lose this
And torture chambers, extermination camps,
Knives and strangling hands, mass graves,
Garrotting wires, bullets, bombs, papers
Issuing orders, canisters, bayonets and battle-fields,
All our extravagant malevolence would be excised
As cancer. Not just evidence but the implements
Of the act in motion gone. "I will not hold
In being the hand that stabs, the member that
Rapes, the brain that hates." I see now it was not
Christie God honoured when He created each
Moment of that bone in existence in its place
All those years but the human race. And I suspect
His hand was too steady for my liking.

Man of Love

That man of love the Christians call God,
Who does his dirty work on the fateful day?
Are henchmen seraphim in stylish uniforms
Assigned the job at the end of the railroad?
All "Schnell schnell! Here for the hospital, here
For work." Or does he take responsibility?
Will the man of mercy look me in the eye
When I reach the front of the queue
At the head of that vast cliff and pitchfork
And prod me into the molten lake below?
Will he close his ears to the first hundred,
The first million, or will he grit his teeth
To the holy work and hew the billions?
Perhaps he'll take the easy way and wish
Us straight inside the pit, insulated
For sound, and pretend for all eternity
He does not see or hear. Heart growing
Harder, mind madder, God with His fingers stuffed
In His ears, eyes squeezed shut: "la la la" rising
To a shriek of unknowing. Or slice out tongues
No longer needed for the everlasting dirge.
His love, a many pincered thing.

Confession

"Listen!" whispers the cleric.
"Between friends, I have worshipped,
Studied and prayed my whole life,
Sought God with all my being.
I see now it's a lie. We are free."
"What do you mean?" said the man.
"You can do anything you want.
Shape your life as you think fit."
The man struck down the cleric
And left him for dead. For he was
Terrified to hear such words.

Fox

I look for the myth
But all I see is a
Shabby old fox,
Miserable in the rain.
For a few weeks
He's taken to sleeping
At the base of next door's
Cherry tree. God knows
Why. It's cold and
The grass is damp.
There's no shelter
Beneath the leafless
Canopy. If it were me
I'd be snuggled in
My den under ground.
Now I see he's limping,
Holding his front paw
In the air. And
He's trapped by the high
Fortress fences
Of our garden.

He stands in the bedding
And looks up longingly
Then tests elsewhere.
"I'm calling the RSPCA."
But while I'm looking
For a number
He finds a way
Under the fence
By the front gate,
Out into the street
And away. He could
Never know that warmth,
Safety, food, compassion,
Healing were so close.
And yet, the distance
Was as far as language:
"Wait there. Someone's
Coming."

Erdogan the Fool

Just another thin-skinned tyrant,
An ass braying its own importance.
*"How dare you! I've won elections.
I'm democratically legitimate."*
But, Recep, illiberal democracy is democracy
With a hand at its throat, throttling,
Crushing the windpipe.
*"Know your place! You're no one.
Who are you to lecture me?"*
Know yours! Here's a lesson
In civics for Erdogan the dunce,
Stand in the corner and recite:

caesar must render unto Us
For nothing is caesar's.
Power flows not from
caesar to the People,
But from the People to caesar,
Ours to give, Ours to take.
Power is not *for* caesar but
For the People. caesar is
A servant, nothing more, and

A servant must know his place.
We may ridicule Our servant,
Question him, send him
packing. He is no one
Special; We are special.
Our servant is not above
The law that We are not above.
He has no rights that We
Do not give him. He is one
Of Us put in place for a short
Time to get things done
That We wish to be done.
If he steals from Us that which
We do not willingly give
We will not forgive and he
Will never rest. For We,
We are the People, and
We are sovereign.

"Fatima," I say, "what do you think
Of Erdogan?"
"Who?"
"Erdogan"
She looks bemused.
"Your president."
"Oh!" she smiles.

"We say 'Erdwan'. It's difficult.
If I say against him he'll sue me."
"Doesn't he understand
He's a servant of the people?
You have a right to criticise your
Servant." Obviously not.
She smiles again,
Almost apologetic.
I say I was angry about
The attempted coup. It was
A mistake. Now he'll take
The chance to move against
All his enemies, even those
Who are legitimate.
"That's what he's doing.
All his opponents."
"Will democracy survive
In Turkey?"
Before she speaks it's time
To let the students in for their
Exam. But I know the answer.

Fethullah Gülen, anyone who
criticises is Fethullah Gülen.
It's the TV villain method of attacking
Freedom: pick an enemy,

Any enemy, shuffle the pack.
And look, every time I pick it out.
It's magic!
Let me acquaint you with the
Rest of the lexicon:
"Human rights are a luxury
We cannot afford."
"We must have order!"
(Bonus marks if said
With German accent).
And don't forget to claim
Everyone who dares speak
Against you is "working for our
Enemies". You picked Fethullah
Gülen but there are plenty
Of standbys. Immigrants, Jews,
Kurds, the West. Anyone, really.
Just keep saying it over
And over… Here's some
Advice from a man named Joseph:

"If you tell a lie big enough and keep repeating it,
People will eventually come to believe it.
The lie can be maintained only for such time
As the State can shield the people from
The political, economic and/or military consequences

Of the lie. It thus becomes vitally important
For the State to use all of its powers to repress dissent,
For the truth is the mortal enemy of the lie,
And thus by extension, the truth is the greatest
Enemy of the State."

Dissent, the very heartbeat of democracy,
Of freedom. Democracy is built on
Disagreement. Men are contrary, see things
Differently. The absence of dissent is
The sure sign, the symptom of tyranny,
Of illness in the body politic. The anti
Bodies keep us well. The dissident
Is hero of our world.

I stand with Ball, Locke and Pankhurst,
I number myself with…
"Pankhurst? A woman?" He sneers.
"You cannot put women on an equal
Footing to men. It is against nature."
Is that right, Recep? Well, here's a kick
In the teeth. I know many women who
Are superior to you, cleverer, more creative,
Wittier and, let's be honest, better-looking.
So if you are inferior to those who are
Inferior you must be nothing much at all.
Quite an admission.

Erdogan, the pompous, primping, preening fool,
Who would serve that man a cup of tea?
Not I. Though dictators are never friendless,
They have their useful idiots.

The shame of your nation. I imagine Tenzile
Lying exhausted having splashed you out.
An angel appears out of heaven:
"THIS IS WHAT YOUR SON WILL DO TO
FREEDOM IN YOUR LAND." She observes
The future horrified, and understands she's given birth
To a parasite, a thing lower than a paedophile,
For such men steal the future of some children; you
Steal them all. She grabs a pillow and smothers
You and rejoices for she's done a righteous thing.
I imagine a better world.

Keep going on this path, Recep, and be a dwarf
Beside Mustafa Kemal Atatürk. And remember this:
A tyrant's grave is for dancing on.

Two Men

Two men rest their bones
And warm themselves around
The fire of their friendship.
Around them chill winds howl.
One man thinks:
"I've given more logs to
The fire than my friend.
I won't let him take advantage."
The other reflects:
"I have fewer logs than he.
He should be more considerate.
I won't let him play me for a fool."
There they sit, with all
The kindling they need
To make it through the night,
Watching the flames die,
Hearing the wolves close in.

Cogito Ergo Sum

Most people are not.
They bathe in another man's
Filth and call themselves clean.
Hand-me-down minds:
"See this!" "Hear that!"
"Swallow this!"
Not worth living,
Sneers the Greek.
Kill him for that.
What does he know?
He never slaked himself
From the well of hypocrisy,
Never gorged the apple
Of ignorance, blistering his
Tongue and roof of his mouth.
The children of the Serpent
Forsake him as they must. Strike at
His head but miss, cover their
Heels when you watch.
But look closer and see
How they smile and taste the air,
See how even the lie must be
True to its nature.

Time Plots Against You

From one thing above all
Would I protect you,
But cannot pledge my strength
Against the years. My prayer:
"Let her live long but
Die before me."
May our house swallow *me*
With echoes of our days,
May *I* shuffle scared and searching
For you through rooms teeming with
Us. May *I* stumble through laughter
Leaching from walls we painted
Years past. See you in our garden
Though you're nowhere to be seen.
I fear time plots against you.
I know it. Picking us off
'Til the day no one knows
Your number or finds their way
To your door who isn't
A wolf. Oh, give my heart the strength
To beat one beat past your final
Sigh, is all I ask of life.

What I Should Have Said

"What's so great about democracy?"
He sits back, hands behind his head, smug look on his face.
He's shown what a radical thinker he is, dared to think the unthinkable,
And now he awaits our admiration.
I can hardly believe anyone would say something so stupid, uttered on the calm
Waters of the land that gave it birth but I'm up for debate.
I remind him of Churchill's appraisal: "The worst form of government,
Except for all the others", and that kills the conversation, everyone sitting awkward
Until the talk turns to food and what we'll eat next.
But now I wish I'd said more:
"Then shut your mouth! Because in a dictatorship you wouldn't have the
Right of free speech. Unless of course you think you'd be part of the elite
That bosses everyone else around. Is that it? What's so special about you?"

And there's the rub. He wants a government based not on continual scrutiny,
Even mockery of bad ideas, but on the principle of: "Silence! I'm speaking."
Oh, please, shape our world and let us grovel before your all-knowing
Wisdom. The philosopher said: "Man, ultimately, is the desire to be God."
The desire to be the centre, all eyes fixed admiring, no one saying no.
"What's great about democracy," I should have said, "is that it gives a
Defence against people like you."

When I Think of Giving Up

So easy it would be to lose myself in despair of mankind,
The vile and ceaseless hypocrite, with its mafias, gangster
Governments and insufferable religions. Man was born in
Chains, captured in a social concrete that rarely softens.
We would speak out but it gets in our throats, we don't hear
Or see. We're baked in it. How tempting to throw up my
Hands, to say "let the parasites win the day, the world is theirs
By right of force and numbers". But then I look at you.
Kind, not because some god orders you to be, gentle,
Unassuming, not grasping or ambitious, too good for me.
Without question I would die for you and such as you,
Rare with good hearted innocence, always helping others.
How effortless you make it seem. As effortless as it is
To be yourself. For you, and such as you, it is worth
Fighting to break the chains and shatter that concrete.

This

At the centre of my
Understanding of the
World, this: I shall
Lose everything and
Be destroyed.
It is the nature of what
I am. No God will
Save me, no man
Can save me. I
Have a span allotted
By the working out
Of this universe
And my place within it.
It and I both process.
There was nothing
Of me before the
Process began, and
Nothing of me will
Continue when the
Process of me ends.
How can a process
Survive its own

Conclusion? A
Biological course,
Birth, ageing, death,
No different, besides
Intelligence, from any
Other life form, that also
Has its start and its
End. I hope that during
The time I have I do
Not suffer unduly, and
That I am kind to my
Fellow creatures, human
And otherwise. Most of
All, given that time
Is short and I will know
Nothing of reputation
When I'm gone, I
Hope that I make the
World better in any way
I can for those who
Follow after.

justice for the primate

an alpha chimp ambushed by a rival,
smacked across the head with a stick
from behind. the challenger stands
triumphant, its dead leader's brains spilling
on the jungle floor to feed the ants
and scavengers. there's no justice
for the murdered chimp. one species
alone expects justice after death in
any sense, one species alone goes
to heaven or hell. our souls live
in that fraction of dna that makes
us clever, hairless, and able to survive
the death of our body. yes with cleverness
comes a soul, though it's hard to locate
precisely. but one day things might
be different for our cousins. perhaps
a plague will wipe us from the earth,
or war. and the aeons will cover our
cities. then perhaps the chimps will take
their place on a higher rung of jacob's ladder.

with a bigger brain they'll think they were
created special, different from all other animals,
immortal, chosen. god will speak
to some of them, prophet chimps,
who will be above criticism and will tell
other chimps what to do to save
that small fragment residing in their dna
from the flames.

Cold Universe

This is a cold universe,
Its stars feeble and far apart.
"We demand justice!" cries the man.
Justice!
Jackboots shiver in the morning air,
Doors shatter.
Whisper men, your servants are
Listening. Hide, they are watching.
"You work for us. You understand
That, right?"
He winks and slaps his baton
In his palm, not even conscious
It's there.
"Anything you say, boss."
"Love conquers all," they cry.
The parasites cover their mouths,
Bodies convulsing.
"It certainly does," replies the conman
Solemnly.
"No arguments here," says the thief.
"Love above all things," intones the
Psychopath.
And politicians add to their stockpiles,
Just in case.

Such Sustaining Glimpses

How dare I write a poem
About my fear of death,
Or the daily small observations
Of what it is to live my life?
How dare I write of daffodils
Or pike, or the truth of beauty,
Of rain or sudden moments
At railway stations? I am
A war poet. I cannot afford
To be sentimental or obscure.
I live in a world of mass
Graves and the Klan,
Of daily rape and murder, of
Men who think they own countries
Because they do. I live in a world
Ravaged by fabrications that
Enslave, by the stupidity of cruelty
And the cruelty of stupidity.
And I am at war with these things.

What hope is there? Freedom
Has never been the natural state

Of men. The sheep long for
Wolves. You hear the blithe
Confession of the halfwit:
"I'm not interested in politics."
Then shut your mouth and get
You to the fields to chew your cud.
Methane and milk is all you're
Good for, your children for the
Sunday roast!

All is politics!

The food you eat, the water
You drink, where you go, where
You cannot go, what you say, what
You cannot say. Freedom is a muscle.
But God loves idiots and beetles,
Scurrying around, rolling their dung,
Shaping a world for coprolites,
Putin, Erdogan and Assad.

Yet even in war the sun
Breaks through clouds and
Lights up pools of water in the
Shell-cut craters. And I remind
Myself, it is such sustaining

Glimpses that makes the
Fight worth while.

Good Question

"You do all this writing.
What's it for?"
Ha! Most days
I wonder the same thing.

This Paradise They Dream Of

This paradise they dream of,
What place is it? For some
A garden, for some a city,
For me a beach of sand and
Dunes, deserted but for you
Who hold my hand and keep
It warm, and laugh as spray
Splashes and the wave crashes
High up the shore chasing.
Not a soul but us, that's a paradise
To dream of, and the thought of
Snug evening seclusion, our
Table laden, heaving, deep aromatic
Wine, and all the conflicts of
Those future denizens far distant.
Paradise is a place I've been.
I know the route. But without you
I can't get there.

Peccadilloes

Far enough away, nearly a rumour,
Perhaps I'm small enough to defraud
Him and still escape notice. Too much
Weight, the odd cigarette, or some other

Risky behaviour. A man must have
His peccadilloes. But all the time I'm
Uncomfortably aware I leave scent
Marks in the woods, rubbing raw meat

Against trees and hoping the
Grizzly has a belly full as he passes
By. Why do it? Why play the prodigal
When a single throw could squander

The lot? Am I mad? "You can't hoard
Life." I know this. Stick it under a mattress
And it starts to smell. But like a beggar
With his lottery loot I'm giddy. I dance beneath

The canopy and shout: "Come and get me!"
Then skip behind the nearest tree,
Holding my sides, stifling a howl, sneaking
A peek to see if he's there. Perhaps

It's a game of hide and seek that's
Lasted too long. I want to win, of course,
But it's no fun just hanging around, stuck
In a cupboard at the far end of the house,

Simply sitting there, like life in a traffic jam,
Or an open-plan office. A life of tedium
Is a misnomer. I want him in the room,
I want to behold that carnivore through

A crack as I hold my breath, and marvel and
Quail. I am the fox that spurns its stash
In favour of the lion's kill. I want to steal
From beneath its nose and feel its hot breath

On my back, its claws lunging and swiping
Air, its teeth snapping on its tongue. I want
To dance away as it stands, panting, staring
After me, knowing that I beat it.

At least for today.

A Moment Ago

The story is meant to be:
We're on our way for a few
Days' holiday. We planned it,
Paid money for it. It didn't
Need to happen. We could
Have gone elsewhere,
Or stayed home. There was
Nothing inevitable. A moment
Ago we held hands, talked of
Things we'll do when we land.
Now terror. And I'm aware
You will die. If only I could
Get back to that moment before,
That safe place. But
It's gone, and I can only sit
And scream as the world
Plunges away, and that
Feeling in my stomach,
And blind hope, and certain
Knowledge, and I can't
See you, and waiting
For forces that will scatter
Me in bits, and all I want is
That you won't die.

In the Garden with You

We sit not talking in the garden,
Sun on our faces and necks.
A crow location-bleats as it
Goes over. A blackbird sings
In the giant oak by the railway
Line. A bumblebee, first of
The year, gorges on Aquilegia.
We sip tea and smile. I stroke
The tips of your fingers,
Breeze strokes your hair
And makes an offering of blossom.
Clouds, white and grey, slip by,
Convoy to a new world. And I
Wonder, what if there is no
Grand meaning? What if life
Is simply a tapestry of moments?

The Life That Matters

I used to think
Life should be used
To make art.
Now I see
Art is to make life.
Not artificial, not contrived.
That is to get it wrong.
But deeper, wiser, better.

S.M.

"We didn't have sex, you know."
I found it odd she needed to say this.
I was there, not having sex with her.
That not having sex, together with
The kiss we did have, keeps her
Fresh, young and beautiful.
She's frozen in that time. It's
Heat that turns things rotten.
Now I can hear her laugh, see
Those eyes and lips, her hair
So glossy, when all else has
Faded. A flash from those eyes,
I was hers. Though the chains
Fell away long ago, I still wear
The manacles.
How can not having sex
Be such a big deal?
How can not eating be a
Big deal? A few days you'd
Remember, a few weeks a
Defining event. Two years I

Saw her daily, her flirting an
Aroma that drove me to distraction,
Salivate and whine: "Give me
Your paw", "roll over" – anything.
I would have done anything.
But a slave cannot be a master.
A harsh lesson for a silly boy,
One I needed to repeat before
It took. My great sorrow as I
Look back now, a flabby, myopic
Fifty-year-old man, is not that
We did not have sex, though I
Wish we had, but that I'll never
Feel intoxication like that again.

Of Paradise

Paradise would be paradise
Without people.
But not without birds.

A World Unblinking

And will there exist
In the paradise so soon
To come, the unsleeping,
Unerring, unyielding,
Eternally focussed,
Undistracted, Remorseless,
And precise paradise to come,
An algorithm of kindness?

Fire in My Lungs

Caught at the bottom of the sea
Mouth clamped tight.
"You must breathe," they say.
"It is life," they say.
I am afraid. There's fire
In my lungs. I ache to
Do what I must not,
The thing that will
Make me like them.
Forced to it should I
Pay the penalty?
Where shall I launch
My appeal? And how,
Being dead?

What is poetry?
Simply this, language distilled.
Careful.

What They Cannot Imagine

The young look at the old
And the middle-aged
From the blaze of their
Passions,
And cannot imagine fire
Where they see only embers.
Who could desire those rolls
Of fat, those scrunched faces,
Aching backs and knees,
Bunions, toe nails like hardened
Steel, liver spots, wasted muscles,
False teeth and stale breath?
"Like kissing a tortoise." And yet,
Locked in their frenzy of desires,
Infatuations and lusts, they cannot
Imagine their Romeo, their Juliet,
Will someday likewise be less
Than perfect. Don't they know
Fire consumes? But it also
Transforms. For the lucky ones,
Those who add the catalysts of
Kindness and patience to the mix,

A different burning marathon-love
That is deeper, wider and more
Wonderful than anything they feel
Now. But this they cannot imagine.

The Question They Hate

Human beings killing
Each other on a vast
Scale, and all because
Some had the temerity
To ask: "Who put you
In charge?"

The reply, guns
Brandished in the faces
Of kids, electrodes
Thrust at genitals, finger
Nails ripped, the ingenuity
Of man at its pitch.

And the word 'terrorists'
Bandied so glib, a soiled
Bandage sullied with gore
And brains. Is there
Anything more revolting than
The indignation of tyrants?

Here Be Monsters

I'm drowning in bullshit.
Not just alternative facts,
Deliberate lies men dress
As truth and send to the pageant.
That's bad enough, the lie
Giving truth a helping hand.
But self-deception. Is it just
Mental laziness? Too much
Effort to go through life actually
Using the mind?

"You're so superior, Andreas!"

That's my fear. Wafting around
In a cloud of smugness, like a
Fart that won't dispel. But it isn't
Like that. I just want to know
Where I am. What's the use
Of a map if it only ever tells you
You're where you want to be?

That man, did he really believe
He'd be given seventy-two doe-
Eyed virgins and eternal bliss
For stabbing a policeman and driving
Into a mother fetching her kids
From school? Is a man on holiday,
Celebrating his wedding anniversary,
A target for goodness to kill?
The stench is overwhelming, like
Living in a latrine. And it begins
With the questions we don't ask.

Lucky

*"This is where we're thinking
Of putting you. Have a look
Round."* And he saw leaves in
Autumn, shivering in woods,
A bear by a lake lapping and
Ambling, testing the air, an
Eagle circling at the limit of
Sight, and sheer rock face
Hidden by cloud and the steam
Of falling water. He saw a
Figure, alone, watching the bear
Then climbing upwards in the
Free air. Now he was gliding
Above a plain. Wolves chasing
Bison, grass swishing and
Hissing in the wind. He saw rain
And the freshness after the rain.
Coming closer a flower burst
Open for the first time, and
He heard the stop−start of
Bees in a meadow. And
The air filled with summer

Song of blackbird and robin
And thrush. Now the ground
Was covered in snow, and
Bare trees stood sentinel.
A stone church, a graveyard,
A lane. Smoke spiralling
From cottage chimneys and
A dog barking excitedly
Somewhere close. There's
A beach in a storm, waves
Smashing, and the same
Beach on a windy sunny day
With men and women racing
Horses, whooping and laughing
And yelling. Gulls soar and
Scream and he squints at
The horizon. How big is
The sea, he wonders? And
Finds himself on a ship,
Dolphins taunting the prow.
"You can swim beneath these
Waves, you can fly above
The ship. It is an astonishing
Place."
"And I can come here?"
"Today, if you'd like."

Fifty years later he died of a
Heart attack from fat clogged
Arteries, after years of staring
From the same window of the
Same drab office. "There has to
Be something more," he'd
Sigh before adding: "No, you're
Right, of course. I'm lucky
To have a job like this."

If You Can Believe This

God loves me.
Not that part of me
You can touch.
That may be starved
Or smashed, sliced
Or crushed. God
Does not love that.
He'll let that rot.
And not that part
Of me that thinks
And feels and decides,
Not my mind.
That does not survive
Alzheimer's, never
Mind death.
The part of me
That God loves
Is 'soul', an
Undetectable self,
Which contributes
Nothing to what
You would call me.

That is what God
Loves, and what will,
(If I come to conclusions
Of which He disapproves)
According to his servants
On Earth, burn forever.
Together with billions
Of other souls, which
He also loves.

there are good days

the milk sours in the baking sun,
and the food caddy writhes with maggots,
which i kill with bleach. by my
car a rag dried with blood which
i kick away. i'm suffocating in this heat.
i look up and see a pigeon, desiccated,
caught by its wing in metal mesh
put there to keep it out. i'd feel pity but
i'm too disgusted. i want to pick a fight.
i see a pregnant woman and i think
"it's a trick and it gets us all", none of
us immune. an infected bite that eats
its way through our bodies, into the blood
like sepsis. i want to escape, but i also
don't want to. there are good days.
but i'm under no illusion. i see my father,
brain riven with malevolent fungus
pushing its way in to every moment,
every intimacy, every love, every
lesson life taught him, spilled ink on
the calligraphy of his days, smothering
the life from his life till soon he'll just

gape and stare. i see my mother –
diabetes, under-active thyroid, atrial
fibrillation, old age. i have a rich
inheritance. her nimble intelligence
now reduced to stumbling, stuttering
torment. "i don't know where dad
and i would be without you". i do,
why do you think i'm still here?
i see sara, and i think of the ways
i let her down. so much hope, my
little ballerina, so much vim and talent,
but this is a universe of entropy,
decay is our master and the day
looms when she'll struggle to stand.
"you're a bundle of laughs today,
andreas!" well, that's what happens
when i forget my pills. but i look
at her and i feel sad. one day i'll hold
her hand and watch the life go from
her eyes, or worse, i'll leave her lonely
and afraid while i moulder in dirt.
who will look after her then?
there are good days, yes, but more
at the beginning, and they, like all
things, will have their end.

Plagued

I can't think, my mind is plagued by
Images I don't want and wish would go
Away. You know the ones, you have
Them too. Even at my age it doesn't
Take much to set them off. Almost
Anything will do.

And then I hear: "Lust is a sin. Repent."

What a massive bloody cheek!

Biology generates these thoughts,
They slop into my mind all day long.
Chemicals, DNA, the way the brain
Is wired. If it were up to me I'd have
A little switch somewhere discreet –
It's much to be desired –

And only feel the urge on the odd occasion
I turned it on. Once every couple of weeks
Would be fine by me. Think of the time
I'd save. But I'm built in a particular way
That doesn't suit me one bit and then reviled
When I don't behave,

Threatened by the God of misery as though
He had nothing to do with it. But then again,
Perhaps He hasn't. The other explanation
Makes more sense. So don't tell me I'm
A sinner when I have feelings I can't help cos
That's just nonsense.

Slipstream

Did you know that, if Trump wins, on his inauguration then his first day in office he will be 70 years 7 months and 7 days. 777 is a prophetic number and my belief is God is placing him there for a much bigger purpose.

We are in the slipstream of stupidity.

*The Holy Spirit spoke to me and said,
"Trump shall become My trumpet to the American people, for he possesses qualities that are even hard to find in My people these days. Trump does not fear man nor will he allow deception and lies to go unnoticed. I am going to use him to expose darkness and perversion in America like never before, but you must understand that he is like a bull in a china closet.*

We are in the slipstream of birds flying arse-first.

I was NOT an original Trump supporter, however, I have come to learn after listening to so many prophesies that God DOES have his hand on DJT! You, of all people, who are studying the Bible, KNOW about CYRUS, DAVID, SAUL OF TARSUS, etc. were used for God's purposes! God can even use a donkey.

We are in the slipstream of donkeys.

Forged of Steel

When stupidity looks
In the mirror it's always
A clever face that looks
Back. The dull eyes
Gleam, the gawp is
Transformed into the
Gaze of one who knows.
Stupid opinions are
Forged of steel and
Last forever, impervious
To doubt or questions.

Teeth for Your Heels

It is not the wolves that defeat them;
It is lack of brains and courage.
Stand and fight, oh bison, stand
And the wolves starve. Death
Has teeth only for your heels.

my country right or wrong

i am my country as much
as those leery-eyed liars,
those stealers of our destiny.
"these are english actions,"
they say. "you must own
them too or be reviled as
traitor to your people. each
crime of ours is your crime,
each lie your lie. it is
england you betray if you
denounce us." but i am
another england, more
noble, a higher, better thing.
i may see further than your
myopia, i may choose for
myself, i may think my own
thoughts and speak my own
words. i may give where you
take. you are england, yes,
you are the worst of england.
and the best is no traitor to
the worst.

Dark. Naked.

We are naked. It is dark.
I hold you in my arms, your
Face against my chest.
I feel goosebumps in your skin
And the solidity of bones in
Your flesh. Your face is wet.
"Shhh," I say in your ear.
"I've got you. You'll be fine."
Around us, other bodies
Press. Buttocks rub against
Me, arms, backs. A sour smell
Hangs heavy in the air.
People moan, whisper, reassure.
A voice rings out:
"God is mighty. Nothing can
Stand against Him." And
Again, and again: "God is mighty."
I try to fend off the crowd, to
Use my body as a shield.
An angry voice: "Can we have
Some room here? There's
A ninety-year-old woman being

Crushed." Children are crying.
"What's taking so long?" says
A man. "Maybe they've run out
Of water," replies another.
"So much for German efficiency."
Laughter, then a faint hiss.
I brace, expecting cold, cold
Water on my skin, but instead
Only a strange smell.
A stinging, burning, instant
Revulsion. Screams and
Coughs. Bodies surge,
I feel you convulse. I lose
My footing, put out my arms
To steady myself,
And in that moment
You are gone.
My throat has closed. Air.
I lunge forward blindly, trying
To reach a wall, a door,
To claw my way out. I claw flesh.
Part of me thinks of you still.
I know you are dying somewhere
Near. I know you are one
Of these bodies I am ripping
Through as I make for the door,

Or treading on. I feel a head
Beneath my feet, small, like
You. Or a child. Air! My eyes
Stream. I fall. My hand under
Foot, ground into concrete.
I scream a screamless scream.
Lake of fire. Mercy.
Lungs sucking acid.
Air! "So it's now,

What We Truly Are

Why don't we fear the slow-motion death
Of everyday life? It's what we're used to,
Is that it? Cellular replacement of self.
One for one until what's left of that authentic
Squalling child? Why don't we fear the
Ceasing of conscious mind, our daily plunge
Into an icy tide that never drags us out to the
Depths, until suddenly it does?

We die daily.

Am I my memories? If so, which ones? Not
Two days in a row have they ever been the
Same. Which set brings me closest to
Myself? The death of which memory spells
The end of me?

"You're a libertarian," says a friend.

I bask in the word and determine it must always
Be so. How could I be otherwise? But the
Monk of my teen years and I share a sullen

Silence, each appalled by the other.

"Where did I go wrong?" he asks.

What was the moment I pushed away from the boat
And struck out for shores unknown?

"Christ died for you!"

Will he go to Heaven and I to Hell? We share
DNA and some memories, but are not the
Same. Perhaps God will untangle me,
Separate wheat from the chaff of this single
Lifetime. He shakes his head. I have condemned
Him, cut him off from his Saviour. A fate
He never contemplated. Ah, never say never.
That is the lesson I've learned. Just keep running
After those nimble feet disappearing into
The thicket and you'll be faithful to yourself.
The only faith that matters.

All those deaths we do not fear. Why then are
We terrified of Death? It must be the break
In the process of self that is ground zero.
It is the locus of the loss of self, and it tells
Us what we truly are.

Flame

A girl stands in the darkness
Holding her grandfather's hand.
They stare at a candle.
"Where does the flame go?"
She asks. The old man smiles.
"Nowhere," he replies. "A flame
Is a process. When a process ends
It doesn't go anywhere. It simply
Ends."

Signifying Nothing

Yesterday's world
Is ashes.
Today, as yesterday,
I stand beneath
The branch and listen
As the blackbird
Sings.

PART II

LET MY PEOPLE GO

"The only way to deal with an unfree world
Is to become so absolutely free that your
very existence is an act of rebellion"
                          Albert Camus & Raif Badawi

I

The Three-Headed Monster

Christianity, Islam and Judaism,
Three turds from the same arse,
That tribal martinet usurper of an
Entire universe. Tragedy or farce?

Go on, go back to the desert. Speak to
The prophet who doesn't even know
To wash his hands after defecation.
This is your fount, your mouthpiece, or so

The clerics would have you believe.
He points to the sky with wide eyes:
"We are the centre of the universe!"
He boasts. And you shake your head at his lies.

"No. No, you fucking ignoramus, we're not!"
You want to yell. But you're too polite.
He lowers his voice, leans in:
"God speaks to me," he confides. Is that right?

So why did He take the trouble to hide
Himself, the ground of all reality, the essence
Of all that is, just so he could speak
To some twat in the desert? It makes no sense.

But what does? "I'll make a world of men
To judge, but first it's my divine will to waste
A hundred million years on dinosaurs that
Have nothing to do with anything. Haste

Is for mortals." A hundred million years of
Trillions of lives that are utterly beside
The point – not even mentioned in infallible books.
It looks suspiciously as though we've been on a ride.

And what of the schizos in those twilight days?
Padded cells and pills were thousands of years
In unforetold future. Perhaps their voices
Divided to demons and God, depending who hears

Violence, who peace. Modernity taking instruction
From a blend of ignorance, poetry, and insanity.
A touch of literal-minded doctrine that gives
An infallible recipe for inhumanity.

"I'm not brainwashed!" you insist. Oh really?
Your claim's the very definition:
"Nothing you say will change my mind!"
A gull's sure belief overpowering cognition.

"But these are religions of mercy and love,"
You plead. And the earth cries out with the blood
Of the billions murdered on behalf of the glowering
God who set a precedent with a flood.

II

God rubbed his eyes and squinted at his alarm clock.

"DO YOU KNOW WHAT TIME IT IS?" he
thundered

"Sorry," said the troubled believer: "It's just – that Noah business. You know, the flood."

God plumped a couple of clouds, sat up: "YOU'RE A REAL DOG WITH A BONE, YOU KNOW THAT? MAKE IT QUICK. I'VE GOT A BILLION THINGS TO DO TOMORROW."

The man frowned, nodded. "Can we just run through it one more time?"

"I TOLD YOU. MANKIND WAS UP TO ALL SORTS OF DEPRAVITY. IT HAD TO STOP."

A pause. God's eyes closed, His head dropped.

"Surely not the kids though?"

God jerked awake, a pained expression on His face. "KIDS? OF COURSE NOT. BUT MY SERVANT AMALRIC HAS THAT COVERED. ANYWAY, I CAN ALWAYS MAKE MORE."

"It's not very merciful though, is it? Or good? Or just?"

God sighed again and nodded. "I MUST ADMIT I FELT A BIT BAD ABOUT THAT ONE," he said. "THAT'S WHY I INVENTED THE RAINBOW."

"So you altered the properties of light to show that you wouldn't flood the entire world ever again?"

God brightened. "YES! THAT'S IT."

"But you never actually flooded the entire world, did you? There's no evidence in the geological record for that."

"WELL, IT MAY NOT HAVE BEEN THE

WHOLE WORLD, BUT IT WAS VERY BAD... EXTENSIVE."

"So you altered the properties of light to create the rainbow in order to promise never to create a very bad, extensive flood again?"

"NOW YOU'VE GOT IT!"

"But haven't there been loads of those? What about Katrina? The Indian Ocean tsunami?"

God looked concerned. "LOOK, I'D ANSWER, BUT YOU'RE ABOUT TO HAVE A HEART ATTACK..."

III

Tell me the stories of Hell God I love to hear.
Things I would ask Him to tell me if He were here.
Scenes by the fireside, tales of the pit,
Stories of torture by that malevolent shit.

IV

The God of Love in All His Glory

The gays, I hate them.
I made them so you
Can hate them too.
I made them to hate them.
I want them to hate themselves.
And then I'll burn them forever.
I hate unnatural things. Don't
Fly or watch tv or use a phone,
There's room in hell for you too.
Forget about love – I made sex
For procreation. I hate the childless.
I gave you a brain but don't
Question, don't think.
I hate that. I am God of
Infinite universes but somehow
I have a small mind.
I hate you if you don't believe
The right things about reality,
But I've hidden myself to make
It tricky. Most of humanity will
Go to hell. They disgust me
And I hate them. It will be my
Pleasure to inflict agony forever.
A few will live in heaven, but I'll

Sear their loved ones in
Fire to make sure their heaven
Is hell. Only the psychopaths
In paradise will lead blissful
Lives contemplating the screams
For mercy, unending torture of
Others. I like psychopaths
Who believe the right things.
Heaven is for them.

V

religion of peace

peace if you don't think
peace if you obey
peace if you know your place
peace if you're not gay

peace if you hold your tongue
peace if you don't leave
peace if you don't criticise
peace if you believe

VI

Honest Belief

When a man says:
"I believe!" he tells you:
"I don't *know*!"
When a man who tells you
He doesn't know
Says that he's certain
Then he's brainwashed
Himself. Honest belief
Admits: "But the opposite
May be true."

VII

And God looked on with pity
At a man's agony two thousand
Years ago, stapled to a tree,
And wondered how men could think
This squalid act of brutality
Was His solution to the
Horrors of the world.

VIII

they are wicked and must
be punished. i will punish
myself instead. then i can
forgive them. but most will
still go to hell to suffer at
my hands for all eternity.
this is my great plan.

IX

Point! Point your finger, Asma.
Tell me of the man of mercy,
Asma, the man who had you killed.
Your cry sounds through centuries:
"Murderer! Assassin! Liar!"
You were right about the man,
Too afraid to let you live.
Let me draw you a picture
Of this man, this holy man,
This man of peace, who sent
A soul without eyes to kill a woman.
Oh brave warrior! There
You slept with your five children,
An infant at your breast.
Umayr removed the child

Then performed his holy
Deed, his bold deed, and
Came triumphant but troubled
To his master. "Will evil visit me
As a result of this act?" The
Man of Mercy replied:
"Two goats won't butt their
Heads about her."

X

"ours is a god of heaven,"
they say, yet he presides
over hell, his great
creation, home to most
of mankind for ever.
it is a hell god whose
occasional hobby is
titled heaven. "but it's
not our belief" cry the
jews. but the partial,
jealous, angry god
was gravid from the
start, always smiting,
forbidding, punishing.
the two great heresies
just took things to their
logical conclusion.

XI

let me see if i've got this right.
trillions of years just warming
up, exquisite agony, meted out
for honest disbelief. only one
explanation. He must enjoy it.

XII

They don't like questions, they're afraid of questions.
They call it "insulting religion", "blasphemy".
They want to silence you at any cost.
They don't want to think and they don't want you
To think either. Thinking might mean change,
A tidal wave that washes through their lives, and
They are comfortable in their lies. Too lazy to examine
What they insist is truth. "We fear nothing," they boast,
But then you say: "What difficult questions do you
Ask your religion?" And immediately the fear
They don't feel shows itself. "Like what?" they
Challenge, tone defensive, as though no such
Possibility entered their minds. You give some
Examples and rather than answer your first question
They don tin hats and go to war, addressing
Them as though they were your query, relieved
They no longer have to answer the dangerous

Inquiry that might have exposed their frailties.
They say they are people of the Truth, but they
Threaten like liars, they bully like liars, they evade
Like liars, they lie like liars. "I'm not afraid to die!" But
They are afraid to think because *then* they
Might be afraid to die. Forget about death,
You oaf! Start living. Recognise that if God
Wanted certainty He wouldn't have troubled
To hide Himself. This is the starting point,
Don't you see? The ground of reality, the
Beginning of all things, the origin, the source
Must be blazingly apparent unless deliberately
Concealed. So when you meet those men
Of certainty recognise that they are men of
Self-deception, steeped in mere belief when
What is called for is a higher, harder function of the
Mind.

XIII

How Dare You Question God?

When did you last hear a cleric say
"Think it through for yourself"? You
Need guidance from these wise
Men to make sure you don't betray
The doctrines they espouse. "True
Belief" relies on the fallacious lies

Of an appeal to authority. Shrug this
Off and their next line of attack is to smear
You as impertinent for questioning God.
Completely ignore that the question is
Precisely this, whether your fear
Of offending divine will and the rod

Prevents you from divining if their creed
Is merely human construct. Don't you know
You must assume it's so? If you tread
A forbidden path they're freed
From blame when they slander you so
They can save weaker souls. It's dread

They want so buckle up, with their Trojan
Excuse you're on a crash course and their
Conscience is clear. If God says it's fine
Satanic acts become sublime. They're chosen
These divines, justice is caprice, and they dare
Anything, no matter how grotesque. In time

God's will on Earth as in Heaven is all
That matters. Oh, not very encouraging; they
Don't have faith in their faith to encourage
Questions. Instead, they beg them, small
Minds forbidding doubt, which they say
Is sin, integrity is sin, sincerity cannot assuage

The wrath to come. 'Doubting Thomas', 'infidel',
'Child of darkness'. But truth is light and its great
Weapon is the question. And faith is blind;
The blind walk in the dark. So who, after all,
Is a child of right? They tell you you must hate
False prophets but implicit in this they'll find

Is that all 'prophets' must be tested. "Not ours,"
They say, clinging to the exception, "he's exempt."
How do we know it's not *your* prophet who's false?
They try the lie, "deep down you know", so sours
Their declaration of principles. It's beneath contempt
But it's a revelation. The greatest of their faults

Is that they don't care about the Truth if it harms
Their truth. They plug their ears and close their eyes
And cling with all their might to lies. They swallow
Poison and grin. "Have some," they say, and their charms
Persuade you it's nectar from their God. And so dies
Freedom and honesty in this world if we allow.

XIV

> Start with a man who has insights
> Which far exceed his own religion.
> Charismatic, he gains a following,
> Threatens religious authorities.

His ideas are profound and beautiful
And he believes they come from God
Which makes him a prophet. His followers
Believe the same thing. Then this man
Who lived for others, who challenged
Privilege and vested interests is grabbed
During the night, given a show trial and,
Within hours he's hanging on a cross,
Just another cadaver. Their entire
World view shattered, all their hopes
And dreams destroyed by an act of
Outrageous assassination. How
To make sense? How to give
Meaning? What if it's all part of the plan?
What if what appeared to be senseless murder
Was deliberate sacrifice? But what
Would that achieve? Perhaps he's
Taken our sins from us? A mad solution
For man has no such powers.
Then, the leap. If the prophet was more
Than man, which some suspected all along,
What power would be released by the
Death of God? More questions. God can't
Die, the creator of the vastness of all
Things can't be contained in human form.
Unless… Was this the Son of God?
That leaves the Father in the sky, running
The show, impervious to death,

Exactor of justice as his Son bleeds. But
We're monotheists remember?
There's only one God. Father and Son
One? Sounds mad, sounds man-made.
But He's God! All things are possible with God!
So two are one. And there's something we
All understand about a father punishing
A son, even if it was for something he
Didn't do. Then the Holy Spirit joins
The gang. No one's really sure why.
He's vague, doesn't say much
And what He says makes no sense.
But if two can be one why not three?
For some reason, possibly because three is
Symbolic, we stop there for if three
Can be one so can four, or five or a billion.
And so a web of imagination and gullibility
Is spun around the corpse of a poor young
Passionate man who tried to teach a better,
Kinder way of living and ended up becoming
God, although he never knew it.

XV

strange creature

what is this strange creature?
on the front of its head
is an arse; behind it
a face, simpering, dull
eyed. it's holy so what
it says is holy too.
it's perfect so all its
utterances are true.
only, perfection is
the trial that it must pass,
not the starting point you
silly arse. if it lies,
or claims don't stand the test
you know it's one more like
the rest, man-made, false, a
fib, a tyranny to
resist. if it balks or
rages at your questions
you know it fears to fail
the test it sets itself.
and then it swaggers, struts
and drools, so arm your mind
and don't be fooled, and don't
be blind.

XVI

Pretty smug the belief, conceited even,
That the God of all things has favourites
Based on actions of a man thousands
Of years ago. At least, it would be if it were
Devised now. But in the beginning there
Was a tribal god, angry, jealous, a nasty
Piece of work but only one of many, all
Jostling for position, their priests scared
They might lose their living to some
More attractive conceit. Everyone had
Their gods, but then some genius changed
Everything, some genius saw that
There can only be one source of all things.
A new religion was called for without the baggage
Of the old, without the old lies, a new telescope
Of the mind constructed to view into the infinite.
Not the risible pork-hating, misogynist,
Sex-obsessed misery that blighted and blights
So many lives with petty restrictions and
Threats of torture. To Hell with him.

XVII

To Christians, Jews, and Muslims

I do not submit. I do not obey.
I am no slave. I will seek the
High places far from sheep
Who graze, placid and dull
Beneath the greedy eye of
Their watchful master.
"What difficult questions
Do you ask?" I know the answer
Already. They bask in elective
Stupidity, recoil in horror:
"You may not question!
Who are you to question?"
"Who do I need to be? The
Question is its own authority.
Why may I not ask?"
"Because of the flames,
Because of the blade
Of your merciful Lord,
Your forgiving God."
Which is why I don't submit
And never will. Don't they
See, a God who hides Himself
To give them freedom, not
To overwhelm, is not their made-

Up tyrant who demands and
Threatens? Your minds are
What make you human, but you
Toss them away with hardly a thought.
"No matter what anyone says,
It's my faith." I translate to the
Language of honesty: "I don't care
How compelling the evidence, my
Mind is closed." But the books lie;
Your books lie! The man of doubt
Is the man of virtue, not the man of faith.
Rip them up! Pluck them out! Cast them
Away! Be free.
I am a son of the living God.
I show this by my liberty
As you show you're a slave
By the way you grovel and
Obey petty tedious rules.
"Yes, we're slaves of God!"
They cry with pride. I take
Them at their word but answer:
"Then don't presume to speak
To me, a true son of the true God."
Why would God want slaves?
To achieve what? Don't they think it through?
Christians at least made it that far.
Create a universe just for slaves to
Boss and judge and torture? A mad God.

Is God mad? Or was the instinct parental?
But they're grafted to the old root
And can't escape the Hydra. Strike,
Strike at the root! Prune and it grows
Stronger than before, but kill the root
And the whole thing withers.
Religions die. Mithras, Zeus, Odin
Just interesting myths that had
Their day and curled up mortal
After all. I dream of the day when that
Three-headed monster sinks back beneath
The waves and all that remains are
Ripples where once a serpent was.

XVIII

Hypostatic Union

And God became Great Ape.
Blasphemy, you say? As it happens
I agree, though it's your teaching, not
Mine. But let's get one thing straight,
'Blasphemy' is poppycock. Not so
Much criticism of God as criticism of
Your conception of God, which is a
Smaller thing. So let's define it properly
As delusional nonsense and get back

To the ape. He's just defecated and
Has morning breath. He's having a
Bad hair day. I know you don't like to
Hear such things but men are subject
To frailties and by your account that is
What he was. The doctrine of the defecating
God is central to your belief, though not
Much discussed. I'm being indelicate,
I know. Perhaps you prefer the
Hollywood version, where God never
Had spots or colic, never bruised his
Knee or had indigestion. But I want
You to think it through. You're saying
He was fully God and fully not God.
Man is flawed. So your Saviour is
Fully flawed and fully not flawed.
Some feat, even for God! And if
I'm not convinced, if I have doubts,
Why should Hell be dangled over
My head on a horse's hair? Is the
Price of life self-deception? Must
I will myself to believe your dubious
Claims? As if it weren't enough that
You confer divine status on a man,
Must you make God so capricious too?

XIX

Believe!

"*Believe,*" they say. "*You must believe!*"
They command me not to think,
For then I may draw different
Conclusions, and from core to core
Infect with fungi doubt, maybe
Even them. But whether I think or not
I am commanded. What then if
I find their claims wanting? "*No matter.
Believe what you don't believe.
It's all the same to us. Refuse and
You're God's enemy. And His enemy
Is ours.*" A command to dishonesty then
From the children of truth. Dull my mind.
But they always did prefer the halfwit;
You can't be too dim for Heaven.
None of those pesky questions see?
"*You're very free with insults.
But you know they prove nothing, just lower the
Tone.*" True enough, insults are easy
To hurl and I am Olympian. I train daily.
But all the same it isn't libel if it's true.
"Excuse me, but something just doesn't make
Sense." "*Quiet!*" "Why won't you let me
Ask?" "*We're stoking the flames of the ninth*

Circle just for you." What's so important about
Belief anyway? Why should it make any
Difference? Why does their mad God hide,
Then insist I believe in Him? "YOU HAVE
TO CHOOSE THE RIGHT CREED AND
IF YOU MAKE A MISTAKE I'LL PUNISH
YOU FOREVER." I give up! If you're going
To reveal yourself why not do it properly instead
Of this coy confusing game you insist on playing?
Don't toy with us! But maybe that's all we are.
Tin soldiers to push around. Whisper
Different 'truths' into a few willing ears,
Demand obedience, then sit back as the
Games begin. Who cares if kids get killed?
It's all collateral to those great marshals of
Credulity, the clerics. And when you hold
Your child in your arms and scream at the
Sky they have their platitudes to rub
In like balm. "It's all part of God's Plan",
"They're in a better place", whatever you
Need to hear and makes you shut your
Mouth, and, if anything, strengthens your belief.
Because all that really matters is a different
Cliché. Don't rock the boat.

XX

what puzzles me most
is the way people resist
thinking. according to the
classifieds they're all intelligent,
but i beg to differ. pile high
evidence for evolution;
dna, fossil records, even
antibiotic resistance
yet they prefer to believe
two people once lived
in a lost garden and were
tricked by a snake and had children
who incestuously bred and
formed the basis of the human
race. and their evidence
is simply that someone
wrote it down and attributed
it to god. barnum was right.
what hope is there if they
give their minds up so
easily? is it indolence?
just too much effort to retain
control of their own brain
so they rent it to the highest
bidder? or the first. or perhaps
they don't trust themselves.

they think they've found the truth,
like some plank of wood on the
ocean, and they dare not
ease their grip in case they
topple in and drown. to them
the man who counsels reason
is like some slimy salesman
who turns up at their door
offering snake oil in
return for their souls. *"he's
the one they warned us about,
plug your ears before he says
something!"* to them we're the
ones who've been tricked by
demons, the fools who say
in our hearts there is no god.
but what if we say there may
be god, just not theirs. what
if we pull the wings off their
dogmas; will they still say
they can fly? what puzzles me
is that they don't think it's odd
their religions insist doubt
is sin. what's so right about
certainty? doubtless they look at
the world and say, *"there must be
some meaning to it all. it can't have
happened by accident."* but it can.

it's possible. and even if they're
right it gives no succour to *their*
doctrines, which are flawed as
their creators, and god is nothing
like the man-made creature
depicted in their books.

XXI

They do not stone their women now, the Jews,
And Christians turn from Deuteronomy in disgust.
Both believe their books are God's Word,
But blush for Him, savage yokel. Embarrassed
Eyes turns to Islam. When will Muslims understand
The more they spurn their book the more civilised
They'll become? It's just a knock-off, anyway, from the Jews,
Full of the same bile, the same threats and fulminations,
Even the same stories, though less well told. The
Christians had their chance, though fleeting, to wash
Their hands of the Great Misery and start afresh with
Their God of Love untainted, but discovered that
The sacrifice of flesh needed the Old Man's rage,
Implacable enough to kill an innocent and declare
Justice done.

XXII

Fools and Their Doctrines

They've decided there's no free will
Cos that would infringe on the
Omnipotence of God. Yet they claim
The Qur'an is eternally co-existent.
But that would have forced God's
Hand to create mankind or to be
Absurd. The Qur'an is addressed to
Mohammed and to men. Should a
Book not created by God, but
Eternally co-existent with Him, which
Is in no way a problematic assertion
In itself, address people God
Never created? He would be a
Ridiculous God, though only
He would know it.

XXIII

The Path to the Truth

"What's down there?" you say.
"Nothing that concerns you," growls
The cleric, hand twitching on pommel.

"It's private land." He glares
And you feel the discomfort he means
You to feel. "Who owns it?" You know
You're testing your luck, but why
Shouldn't you ask? He scowls,
*"On your way! You'll get confused
And lost if you go down there. I'm
Protecting you."*
"I'm stupid. Is that it?"
*"You don't have the proper training,
It's not a path for amateurs."*
"Who are you to protect me from
My decisions? What don't you
Want me to see?"
He lurches forward, face in yours,
Features twisted, blade half drawn.
*"We've laid out the road you have to
Take. Do as you're told or…"* he
Looks down at his sword, and grins.

XXIV

Tell me which fits better when you look at the world.
Why are we the way we are?
Are we heirs to a man and woman tricked by a snake
To eat a piece of fruit? Does that explain our depravity?
Flick through the Book of Martyrs, consider devices

That stretch and gouge, burn and prick, hatched in
The ferment of imagination, the tribal loathing that led to
Nazis, the legions of psychopaths.
A million pages could not contain the seething sea of
Hatreds, lies and cruelty.
Imagine now an ape, forged by forces biological,
Limited resources, territorial disputes, breeding rights,
Hierarchy and its privileges, power, survival of offspring,
Terrifying your enemies, terrifying your friends. Consider
The tribe in the next territory invading your land, taking
Its food, enslaving you. Consider doing the same
To them. Pass on your genes. Personal and tribal
Advantage. Are we not ruthless as the nature that spawned us?
It is not in Eden I dig for the origins of envy. I see it gleaming
Now in the chimp's eye that plots. It is not Cain I look to
For murder, but the savage overthrow of a rival for the troop,
An alpha to kill, an alpha to rule, alpha survive and breed.
There's nothing in the apple of this. Nothing of war, nothing
Of cruelty, nothing of power, nothing of us-and-them. Nothing
Of you, and nothing of me.

XXV

Eden

Eden, the great foundation myth that colours everything,
A garden and a con trick performed by a talking snake.
But original sin falls if we evolved. Did Christ die to save us
From nature God gave us, fashioned by our environment?
Only original sin, the shared guilt of a species,
Could act as the root of Christian salvation.
It feeds from this tap root, nourished by an ancient soil,
And dies if the root is severed.

Perhaps it's a metaphor for our own, individual decisions?
Worth a try but the idea each of us has a choice, each of billions upon
Billions upon billions living, dead, through all of history chose sin
Strains credulity. A choice with meaning or value would result in some
At least resisting temptation. But the creed says we're all sinners
Because of a couple of innocents living in a garden. Their 'sin'
Passed to us from Eve, though why is not clear. What, in the
Biological process of reproduction, passes sin from one
Generation to the next? Is sin genetic? Can it be spliced?

But if you swallow it you must swallow it whole, not just the bit you like.
Which means there's a garden somewhere in our world,
A garden guarded by an angel with a flaming sword. Here true
Believers may be tempted to say the 'real meaning' is not literal,

It's an invisible garden, it must have disappeared, or the sword
Is a metaphor. But the point of the sword is to guard it from being entered,
Which would only happen if it could be found.

So where is this Eden? What have we missed? Does it lurk in some
Inexplicably unexplored inch of this ravished world? A pimple of virtue
In the pollution, replete with life extinct elsewhere? Perhaps Tyrannosaurs
Lie down with Triceratops, unaware of their fate in a wide world governed
Now by sin. And does the angel weary of his task? Thousands of years
Just standing there, stupefied, friendless, forgotten, guarding a gate
No one ever visits. Who could blame him if now and then he slips off for a fag,
Or a quick half down the 'Slaughtered Lamb'?

XXVI

Revelation

God messed it up twice before,
That is the essential message of
Islam.

"We say no such thing! It's misrepresentation."

Perhaps you haven't bothered to
Think it through, perhaps
You aren't allowed. Gates of Ijtihad
And all that. So blame Christians
And Jews if you like,
It just goes to show what
Happens when you don't ask
Questions. You have to attack a
Thing from all sides, see if it's
Strong from every angle.

"Blame God? Not us! Not ever!"

Who selected the prophets? Who caused
The books you reject but recognise to be
Written? Who was the poor judge of character?
Doesn't the buck always stop with the
Guy at the top?

Tell me, can the revelations of God be tampered
With? Can any man tamper with the Qur'an?
What was so different about His first two efforts?
Why was only His last revelation co-eternal?

Jews and Christians clung on in the face of
Your Jizya protection racket. Devout
As Muslims, they never needed to
Murder their own kin for apostasy. They
Had more faith in their faith.
So how did they go off message?
Poor planning or poor execution?

Always with Islam you say, "if it's not
Perfect it's not of God." So by its own
Test Islam is not of God.

Twice revelation failed, but you claim He
Came back as a dog to vomit.

He could have created Mohammed in the beginning,
Right from the start. Then there'd have been
Only Islam, with no other creeds confusing and
Drawing away honest men who wanted to do
The right thing.

Oh, it's far from perfect, it's not of God.

Besides, using prophets is senseless.
It sows discord. How many deceivers
Stood before the people? Rightly they
Shake their heads when a new man steps forward
Declaring he speaks God's words.

*"Beware false prophets! They come among
You as wolves among sheep."*

You command the people to discern, but forbid
Them to inquire of you alone, as if they know
The truth before they ask.

*"They do. In their hearts they know. If such
Is Allah's will."*

A counsel of lies. A counsel of madness. The idle
Man, the gull, the fool, gladly follow but the
Wise scent deceit. What have you got to
Hide? Why should I buy sight unseen? It's a pig in
A poke.

Prophecy breeds confusion, accusations of heresy.
Careful now. Honesty is a crime
For which a man may go to Hell.

He could talk to all of us at once.
Easy for Him and no dispute. No religious war,

No doubt or confusion, no Protestant, Catholic, Sunni or Shi'a,
No Gentiles or Jews. Just the people of God.

*"Everyone in the world hears what I'm hearing? No mistake
Then. God speaks."*

Instead, when the prophet choked on poison, hardly anyone
Had heard the message, and since those days most
Men either don't know or aren't convinced.
Far from perfect, not of God.

And what of Hell? It's God's fault so many are misled, so
Why consign them to the flames? People genuinely believe
Whatever they believe. They don't do it to be perverse,
Though that may be the outcome. They search for truth,
But their doctrines say that Doubt, principal servant of
Truth; Doubt, which keeps the mind wide and questioning,
is its enemy.

Surely revelation is of man. We must find The Truth the way
We've found all our truth. Always by questions, always ready
To revise when new and better ideas present themselves.

Men want certainty not maybes. But what if certainty was never
Part of the plan? If God wanted to give us that He wouldn't be
A Hidden God. He wouldn't have banished himself from
Our sight. He is the essence of all things. He took some
Trouble not to blaze before us.

So when your religion tells you not to ask a question, trust that
The brain God gave you is doing what it was designed to do
And ask away.

XXVII

Take It or Leave It

Standing at the top of the mount,
Joshua, great warrior of God,
Leader of Israel, surveys once more
The gift. Face pained, head shaking
In disbelief, squinting skyward,
Apologetic but firm:

"It's not very big, is it? Couldn't we have France instead?"
"Or India?" mutters Caleb from behind his shoulder.
"America!"

The men wait, taking in the plain,
The beauty of the evening sky,
Listening as usual to the silence of God,
But then:

"YOU KNOW, THAT'S PRETTY UNGRATEFUL,"
a voice in the sky rumbles, unmistakably hurt.

Exchange of glances,
Kneeling now, hands grasped in supplication.

"Don't be offended, Mighty One. We are, obviously, totally delighted. It's just, as your chosen people, we thought we'd be getting the best country in the world. Not a tiny one in the middle of nowhere."

A minion creeps forward,
Whispers to Caleb, clatters
Back down the mountain. Caleb,
Face creased in horror,
Whispers in turn to Joshua.

The men grasp each other's arms,
Steadying each other as shock sinks in:
"You're sure? This just gets better and better!"

Shuffling forward Joshua stutters:

"Jehovah, there must be some mistake. There are already people living here!"

A thunderous sigh,
A sudden wind billows
Through their clothes.

"NO MISTAKE. MUST I DO EVERYTHING? JUST KILL THEM AND IT'S YOURS."

Caleb spits a curse, and cowers from expected lightening bolt.

"If you ever change jobs, don't be an estate agent!" says Joshua, too bitter to be afraid.

The wind quickens, drops of water spatter on the sand.

"You promised us a land of our own!"

Disgust falls heavy
As the rain sheeting through the valley.
The men stand, staring into space,
Drenched, indignant, confounded.

"THIS IS IT."

"But, Jehovah, there are people here."

Water blinds their eyes,
Stings their skin,
Suffocates their lungs.
They stagger.
And wait.

"KILL THEM. KILL THEM ALL."

The men grasp each other
And run to a crag jutting from
The mountainside, throw
Arms around it and Joshua
Bellows into the maelstrom:

"You want us to kill babies? But you've only just created them! You must have known this was going to happen! Why make babies just so we could butcher them?"

"TAKE IT OR LEAVE IT," sneers the voice.

But the only reply is
The silence of man
As all Israel turns
And walks back into the desert.

And this
Is the beginning
Of integrity in religion.

XXVIII

Leaving the Land

Behind us only desert. I look back and see
Them toiling on the parched sand, clustered
Round a few putrid pools.
"Come with me!" I call.
They glare. A few rouse themselves to spit
Or shake their fists. A few more come
To the edge of the water and I think perhaps
They will plunge in and join me, but they
Hurl spears and curse. The spears land
With a plop and disappear. I am unconcerned.
We come from water and I see now
The land was a mistake. We gave ourselves
To gravity and now we lumber, flat-footed
And slow in the sand that sucks us down.
We are drowning.
My feet barely touch the sea floor. I am on
Tip toe. I splash forward, salt in mouth,
Spluttering, doing my best doggy paddle.
I laugh.

One day our descendants will glide
Through these forgotten waters.
I do this for them.
Face down I peer into the depths, eyes trying
To focus but see only a few fish, some coral.
My eyes sting. Already they are far behind me,
And I know I will not return. I must swim now
To a new shore where others like me see what
Must be done. A first step back towards our Mother.
Darwin would be proud.

XXIX

The coastal trees buckled and bent in the wind,
And the wind took pity.
"If you wish I will blow from many directions
And you may stand tall like trees in other places."
The trees debated the offer among themselves.
"Why even discuss it?" asked the saplings.
It's obvious we should say yes."
But the ancient trees, fashioned by their burden,
Vetoed the proposal.

XXX

Out of the Mouths of Babes

The crowd threw down their stones and gradually dispersed, cursing among themselves.

A curious boy came over and touched Jesus' hand.

"Master?" said the boy.

"Yes, my child?"

"Are you God?"

Jesus looked about him furtively and whispered: "I am."

He puffed out his chest trying to look bigger.

"I'm confused," said the boy, shaking his head. "You're saying Moses was not your prophet?"

"Not at all!" said Jesus, aghast. "He was absolutely my prophet. I've made that very clear throughout my ministry."

"But you just stopped those people from stoning that woman. They were only trying to do what you specifically commanded through Moses in Leviticus and Deuteronomy. Are you saying you were wrong and for all these years we shouldn't have been killing people for adultery?"

Jesus smiled a forgiving smile. "I'm just saying people shouldn't cast the first stone unless they themselves are sinless."

"I get that," answered the boy. "But why didn't you say that in the first place?"

And Jesus said nothing. For he had no answer.

XXXI

Hallelujah! Belief is a choice!
I used to think it was provisional,
A best guess till verification or falsification.
That was what I believed. Now I know
Better.

"We're commanded to believe!"

I see that now.

*"We believe the Earth is flat. We're afraid
The miasma will take us. The Earth is
The centre of all things because we're so
Important. God made it that way. In a billion
Years our descendants will still be punished
For the act of a man and woman at the dawn
Of time who were tricked by a mischievous snake
Into eating a piece of fruit they'd been told not
To touch. We don't need medicine. If we truly
Have faith God will heal us. We can move
Mountains. Though we never do."*

Do you see now? You go to Hell for making
The wrong choice.

"We believe God chose a confusing, misleading

Way of delivering His message when He could
Have spoken to each of us simultaneously.
We believe we alone are special. We are
Chosen, God's people, and you will suffer agony
Forever. We are glad. Serves you right for thinking
For yourselves and refusing to believe what you
Don't find convincing, even though you're commanded to.
We are vindictive and spiteful, or at the very least
Psychopathically lacking in empathy. Burn: we
Don't care. Burn: the odour of your flesh won't
Reach the halls and gardens of paradise. Burn:
Your screams won't carry on the winds to our
Deaf ears."

It's like the scales have fallen from my eyes!

"We believe there's nothing wrong with the psychology
Of a God who tortures most of humanity while
Simultaneously pampering a chosen few who
Don't care, even though the tortured were friends,
Sons, daughters, brothers, sisters. Even though the
Tortured are people, just like them."

"Some of us don't believe in Hell. We don't think
It's consistent with a loving God. We think all
Shall be well, all manner of things shall be well."

That's just dandy. So you claim God made a mistake,

Do you? Or He allowed His message to be marred
With lies?

Why not just jettison the old religions and start again?

XXXII

How to Slaughter a Pig

A religion is its doctrines. What distinguishes it,
Makes it Judaism not Jainism, Christianity
Not Islam. Doctrine is religion's soft underbelly.

Stab there.

Don't be coy. Rip hard, delve in,
Be indiscriminate. It must all come out, the blood
And the guts and the pus. This is how you slaughter a
pig.

When I was a child
I spoke as a child,
I thought as a child,
I played in the sand,
Built castles against the sea.

But now I see clearly.

Three civilisations built on
A shifting foundation.
Almost a joke, those
Foolish builders.

Their talking snake,
Their world of holy incest
And that miserable male tribal god of
The desert glowering at everything,
A god of mirage and heat.

*"We have the right to believe
Whatever we want to believe."*

Yes you do! It's the right of the
Mad man. And you have the
Right to be mad. State that
As your premise, then
Say whatever you please.

XXXIII

Born of the Bureaucrat

The Christian knows, the Jew knows, the Muslim knows,
They KNOW. Yet each of them knows differently,
Their knowing contradicts. "But I *really* know," says each,

"God confounds the others, tricks them. But to us
He tells the truth." Is that so? Why, then, even within
Each tradition, is there bickering and conflict? Protestant and
Catholic, they know; Shia and Sunni, they know;
Orthodox and Reformed. And all look down on the
Unbeliever, the *infidel*, the only one who has integrity enough
To really question and pick apart the claims, looking for a kernel
Of truth, testing, testing…

This God they know, who speaks to them and holds them
Haughtily aloft, why does He allow this discord if He
Reveals Truth? Doesn't the blood spilled call out
To Him from the filth?

"It's the devil!" they say. "Hurling soil into the eyes of men."
Why then do clerics curse and fulminate when those blinded
Men fail to see what they are told they must see?
All are sincere, all long to be told the truth,
And yet Hell awaits miscalculation.

"God is perfect," they say.
"Is that something you KNOW?" I ask. Some perfection.

I see as never before that the maggot at the heart of
Religion is doctrine. It takes the awe and wonder,
The mystery, compassion, and kindness
And turns it into something born of the bureaucrat.

XXXIV

John Wayne Jesus

God created man in His image,
And man went right ahead and returned the favour.

They refashioned that radical thinker,
The preacher who said, "Go! Sell all that you have and give to the poor. Then come and follow me."

They had to, don't you see?

They'd hate him, *hate him*, the social conservative Pharisees, hate the long-haired hippie pacifist bum so they refashion him to make him one of them. I imagine Jesus turning up on the doorstep of some nice Republican who wants nothing more than to force America to give up its brain and exist on faith alone.

"How dare you? There are plenty of devout people as reasonable as you."

No doubt they're capable of reason, but they choose to abdicate from it. Faith says, "no matter what reason says I believe."
If it were otherwise, if it would not believe unless reason
Could supply sufficient evidence it would not need to make that leap. Faith is blind, remember?

Reason sees.

So, like it or not, faith is unreasonable
Cos it takes the position that reason finally doesn't matter.

Back to Jesus in his rags,
Long, dirty hair, unbrushed teeth
Asking to stay for a few days.
Chances of being let in zero.
Ridiculous that this man is Son of God!
Yet they turn supercilious noses up
At those two thousand years ago
Who took the same view
And you can bet *they'd* want to see
A few miracles just to make sure.

And why not?

Why is it ok for God to hide Himself and allow false prophets to make their claims, then turn up and expect to be recognised without challenge? Isn't the sheer stupidity of this proof enough it's not God? Does he know nothing of human psychology?

"We're not falling for that again. Fool me once… see what I mean? This time we'd like some proof."

But somehow he blags his way in and sets up residence for a few days.

"You're my disciple, is that right?"

"Yes," says the now-uncertain Republican.

"There are poor people in this town
With nowhere to stay tonight.
I want you to let them stay here
For a few days, feed them,
Help them get back on their feet.
Whatever they need."

Is the man mad? Let good for nothing junkies trash my house and steal my things?

The doorbell goes. A young woman, gaudy make-up, low-cut top, short skirt.

"This is Mary; she's staying with us for a while."

"But she's a hooker!"

"That's right," smiles Jesus.

"She's not even an *ex-hooker*. I saw her soliciting down the road last night!"

"She wants to hear my message of forgiveness and compassion… Sorry, is there something in your eye?"

"It's time you met the pastor. You'd be happier staying with him. I've been having Buddhist thoughts recently."

John Wayne Jesus: that's the one they're comfortable with, the one they can live with. He goes around the Middle East kicking the shit out of anyone who disagrees with 'American Values' and sneering at sword control. He preaches love, but not for faggots, Jews and Muslims.

"Love your enemies," he commands. "Then I'll put 'em in Hell."

And secretly they relish the thought.

"Damn them for doing things we call immoral. Things we yearn to do. Things no one would dream of doing with us. Damn them for thinking for themselves. When they burn forever it's what they deserve. Why *should* they think for themselves? We don't."

Love is not tolerant.
Love doesn't try to see the other's point of view.
Love hates gays
And independent thinkers.
Love gives freedom laced with threats,
Love is partial,
It has 'Chosen' people and hates outsiders,

Love is fascist,
Struts around and uses phrases like
"*Our* God is great".
Love burns books, or censors them,
To protect the weak-minded,
Who might otherwise ask questions.
Love is rigid, it is Procrustean,
It doesn't care if its rules inflict pain.
"Marriage is one man and one woman",
Except for favourites like Abraham.
Love makes it up as it goes along.
Love is violent. Holy lands are to
Conquer.
Love is Alpha Male. Women must
Obey, take second place,
Keep their mouths shut.
Eve picked an apple; what more reason
Do you need?
Love loves America most,
Love loves Israel most,
Love loves England most, France most,
Iran, Russia, Saudi Arabia, Greece…
Love is confused.
Love doesn't care that one per cent of
The world's population owns most of its
Resources as long as they throw a few
Bones under the table.
Love stinks.

As they walk to the door, Jesus spots something.

"Is that a gun?" he asks.

"The sacred text guarantees my right to have it," snarls the Republican.

Jesus produces a Bible.

"Show me," he frowns.

"Not that. The Constitution of the United States, Second Amendment."

"You know I'm a pacifist?"

"What about the cleansing of the temple? The den of thieves?"

"I upset a few tables and shouted a bit. That in no way equates to using guns."

Not ok to use a sword to save the person of 'God',
Not ok to use it to save anyone else.
Pacifist Jesus tells us: "who lives by the sword dies by the sword".
But you can set gospel against gospel, and
The flaw in his reasoning is huge. Plenty of

Pacifists have found to their cost they were
Even more likely to die by the sword.
But give the guy a break.
He was only human.

Swords and guns, the weapons of choice for John Wayne Jesus,
But not for the hippie nailed up two thousand years ago.

The Republican looks resigned but then, a moment of inspiration.

"If you're so set against violence, what about Hell?" she crows.

The hippie is speechless. When the religion of a Hell God lays claim to be a faith of love something deeply schizophrenic is going on.

But John Wayne Jesus spits on the floor and glowers: "If you're looking for trouble, I'll accommodate ya."

XXXV

Fair Exchange

Men coagulate around a myth
Like platelets in a scab.
Baby Jesus, God with colic,
Shitting himself and screaming
Through the night. Teenage
Jesus, God with smelly feet
And acne. Don't say it's
Blasphemy, don't show your
Ignorance of what you profess.
It's not polite, granted, like pointing
Out a fart at a dinner party, but
It's doctrine laid bare, literally
What you believe if you believe the
Teachings of the religion.
'Fully man', the second part
Of the equation which somehow
Gets overlooked. Hath he
Not eyes? Hath he not organs,
Dimensions, senses, affections,
Passions, fed with the same food,
Hurt with the same weapons,
Subject to the same diseases?
Prick him, does he not bleed?
Tickle him, does he not laugh?

Poison him, does he not die?
To be man is to be imperfect,
To be God is to be perfect.
He is both, fully, say the
Christians. Careful with that
Stuff; it's holy dandruff, worth
Its weight in gold. Put it over
There with the nails and pieces of the
True cross. We'll sell it to
The brainwashed billions and
Retire, conscience clear, to enjoy our
Lives on some sun-soaked island.
Fair exchange is no robbery.

XXXVI

The Pilate Question

"What is truth?" said Pilate.
What indeed?
Ironic this, as how do we
Know he even said it?
Who heard the conversation
That might record it faithfully?
Jesus too busy being
Flayed and crucified to
Get out his notebook

And jot things down.
His disciples in disarray,
Reduced to prayer and
Lies. Only enemies
Of the ragbag prophet,
Or perhaps Pontius himself
Had a yen for reportage.
"The Bible won't be complete
Without this crucial meeting.
The great confrontation at
The final turning point.
Like Luke and Vader on the
Death Star!"
Belief won't be deterred:
"There must have been a slave
In the room." Sure, perhaps
A slave taking minutes,
Or one who had the chance
To seek out a disciple historian
To write it down decades later:
"I got it all on my cameraphone.
No one looks to see what slaves
Are doing."
Perhaps the motives behind
This risen Lord were baser than the
Salvation of the world. Perhaps
When Pilate released the body
To that rich patron it never found

Its way to a new tomb.
"A resurrection would keep his
Teachings alive. And what
Revenge on the Sadducees
For murdering our master!"
Not the last time in history men lied
In the name of a greater good.
You just need a few peasants
Desperate to feel special for once
In their miserable lives:
"I saw him. He appeared to me!"
A tale to tell for the rest of their days,
The ones who actually met the
Risen Lord before he conveniently
Disappeared. But what does it mean?
If he rose from the dead he must
Have been God! More theological
Reverse engineering. Why allow
Himself to die? To pay for our 'sins',
Like the scapegoat, you know?
But that isn't why he died. He died
Because he was a threat to people
In power. "He used that death to allow
God to punish him." Didn't you just say
He *is* God? "God the *Son*! It was the
Father who punished Him." So there's
A God the Mother too? "Don't be daft.
There's only one God! And He's

Male, all three of Him. And He's so good
He can't forgive without the taste of
Blood." You know you're a lunatic, don't
You?

XXXVII

The Great Conceit

To the Aboriginals of Australia not a word,
To the Picts of ancient Britain, stony silence.
To the Greeks, Romans, Gauls and Egyptians,
To India, China and Japan nothing at all.
But to one people an absurd abundance:
Moshe Rabbeinu, Isaiah, Jeremiah, Hosea,
Amos, Habakkuk… The most conceited of all
Religions, it seems to be. "We are the
Chosen. God holds us special. He gave
Us a Holy Land and bade us exterminate
Every man, woman and child foolish
Enough to think it was theirs already." No
Messengers for them but the blade of
Joshua. And indeed, if the religion sprang
Up now, fully formed, it would be.
But you have to go back, to see how it
Began. One tribal god, just like all the
Others, this one male, a god of war and

Umbrage, petty and resentful. But some
Genius, perhaps the greatest theological genius
Of any age, realised there can only be
One source of all things. And so was born
Monotheism. "There are no other gods
Because there cannot be." But rather than
Begin again on a bedrock of reason insight
Was grafted to faith, universal God and tribal god
Coalesced, commingled, compounded.
Hateful Yahweh, misogynist, irrational god,
Hiding and demanding absolute belief,
Interested only in a fraction of humanity
Until, like some mutating virus it learned
To spread among the peoples, killing
As it went. This was now the God of all things.
A God at war with Himself, a great dividing
God. Why did He not from the beginning send prophets
To every people with His same singular message?
A burning bush in every mountain?
"I Am" everywhere. How much more believable
That would have been than a God
Indifferent to almost the entirety of humanity.

XXXVIII

Dominion

Your sex life is my business
Because the God I believe in
But cannot prove has dominion
Over all things, including you.
This is my belief, and because
I hold myself to be more important
Than you my belief takes
Precedence over yours. I am
Right and you are wrong
Even though I cannot prove it.
I don't listen to your blasphemous
Arguments, not because I'm
Intellectually dishonest but because
You seek to tempt me into doubt,
Which is sin, even though it may
Be honest. And because I know
The truth in my deepest knowing.
I have a greater say about who
You may have sex with than you do.
My God has dominion, so I
Have dominion.

XXXIX

Put Out Your Eyes

*"you must put out your eyes
so you can follow our voice. it is
our religion."*

i seek answers, will you give them?

"yes yes ask what you will," they say.
but see how quick they are to anger.
*"who are you to ask such
questions? arrogant man!"*

*(how dare you ask me questions
i can't answer? how dare you
make me think? how dare you
unsettle my life? how dare you
threaten my world? how dare you
lead me towards doubt? how
dare you show me up when
men look to me for leadership?
how dare you subject me to
uncertainty? and now you've made
me look at a thing i would not
see. i can't answer your
questions and must admit
i don't care about truth or coming*

*with you on a journey
i never wanted to make.
how dare you!)*

who are you not to ask questions?
if it's arrogance to seek truth i
revel in it. pursue the question
to the ends of the earth. it's a
hound crazed with a scent.
call it back it will not come.
you must follow where it goes,
or lose it forever. there you'll find
freedom from lies. is it arrogant to
reject the lie?

*"we have truth already!" they sneer,
"you're misleading yourself, but worse,
you mislead others with your
seditious questions.'*

if you have truth why not
answer me? why are you so
threatened? why so impatient?
it's you who fail to give adequate
answers but won't admit you
don't know. what is it you value
more than truth?

*"put out your eyes and we'll
show you."*

XL

Screaming at the Dock

"Enemy of God!" they scream
At the dock. Not so! Enemy
Of *their* God, made up, small
And fettered by their doctrines,
Petty-minded, male, irrational,
Full of bile and hate, holding
Hell in existence for all eternity,
Expression of everlasting spite.
Presiding over the carnage,
Conceiving torture, cruel, sadistic,
Totally aware of each exquisite
Agony, but somehow still a God
Of mercy. As present in Hell as
Heaven, at one and the same
Moment inflicting pain on billions
And bliss on a lesser number.
Imagine the mind that could
Do this.

"You must think this, you *must*
Believe." Submit to the holy
Lobotomy and be like them.
"Blasphemer!" they rage. Strange,
Their fragile God in need of

So much protection. Delicate
As their injured feelings, the
Unthinkers. Not for them the
Rough and tumble of debate.
"Blasphemer!" when I hear this
Word I know I may as well appeal
To rabies for sweet reason.

"He's a God of mercy," they coo
Over the God of eternal torture.
"He's a God of love," they croon
Over the God who hates billions.
"He's a God of peace," they smile,
And bland grins somehow
Overlook the oppression of half
The human race, the Inquisition,
Witch-burning, protection racket Jizya,
Murder of heretics and apostates,
Extermination of children who lived
In a land 'given' by God. In every
Version the same psychosis
Bleeds through. The psychopath
Bestriding history, up to His neck
In gore and misery.

"That's not our experience. It's not
What we see. Our congregation
Is gentle and kind." Of course it is.

So what? We're talking about the
Truth of reality, not group hugs and
Wishful thinking. Every cult loves
Its own; the brainwashed move
In herds, selective exposure,
Confirmation bias much easier if
I'm not laughing at you and calling
You an idiot. "How do you believe
This stuff? What's wrong with you?"

"Our holy book moves us." I'm the
First to admit there's poetry there.
I'm all for fine feelings and beautiful
Words, but not when they traffic in toxic
Opium. You think it's medicine alone
Sugar helps down? Before they spit venom
They swallow poison.

"We mean only peace to all men."
Then how come you fail so miserably?
"There's a lot of good in our religion."
Yes, and the wife beater really is
A lovely man most of the time. Just
Get to know him, you'll see. But
I can imagine better. I imagine a religion
With no doctrines or duress, full of awe
And gratitude, acclaiming free thought
And the critical mind, the freedom

We were born with to shape our own lives.
That is my creed, and if it's a crime
Then, please, for God's sake, convict me.

XLI

What Has Athens to Do with Jerusalem?

"It's immoral to think for yourself
And you must be punished."
This, finally, is the message
Of the Abrahamic religions.
Don't think! Don't think! Don't think!
Or… "You may think, as long as you
Come to the required conclusion."
If this is true then their demand
Is self-inflicted lobotomy.
If it's not true then their demand
Is irrelevant as there's
No retribution anyway. And why
Should there be for honesty?
"I'm sorry but it makes no
Sense at all." What sort of lunatic
Deity flies into a rage in the face
Of such a statement? "I hide,
I litter the landscape with
Evidence My creation story is a lie,

And then I demand your belief.
What's so crazy about that?"
And the believers plug their
Ears: "It doesn't matter what
You say. My faith is too strong."
Listen to yourselves! You've
Just admitted you're impervious
To evidence that conflicts with
What you want to believe, and
Still you reject the charge of being
Brainwashed. Understand you've
Done this to yourselves. Think
About some of the undeniable
Facts. You can dig them from the
Ground, they're solid, they're real, we
Have their bones. But you still believe
In Adam because you won't question.
It makes you dishonest. You think
Apatosaurus, T-Rex, Stegosaurus and
All those myriad creatures were inhabitants
Of Eden? Humans and dinosaurs
Never shared the Earth; we know it
For a fact; they are far separate in
Rocks laid down millions of years apart.
So Eden must have been after the
Age of the Dinosaurs, but that's not
The teaching is it? Eden was the garden
At the time of creation. Or is that just

Another lie in a book of lies? And what
Of the other men? Neanderthals and
Other members of our genus. Were they
In Eden too? Why were they cast out?
Fellow scrumpers, perhaps? Close enough to
Interbreed, some humans even
Have their DNA, but presumably
Soulless, because the angry, jealous,
Male God is so partial to wonderful us.
The religions of revelation start with a lie,
A talking snake and the founding of the race
Through the incest of the children of Adam and
Eve. Men, blinded by their holy cataracts, go
To any lengths to defend this nonsense,
Though there's no evidence to support it
Except the books they're written in.
But it's not evidence, it's the claim.
Standing against rocks and fossils, DNA,
Textual analysis and sanity. "Believe or
Go to Hell." The counsel of the mad man.
Do we now choose our reality? I shall believe
I'm Croesus and the world is flat; I shall
Believe the Earth is at the centre
Of the universe. To command belief is
Deranged. If it is not so, it is the lie; if it is so,
Why not simply prove it? Why all the games?
"God doesn't want to force your hand;
He wants to give you free will."

"You must believe" is not free will. On pain
Of Hell is not free will. "Give me all
Your money or I'll shoot you," grins the
Robber. "Don't complain; it's free will."
Belief is not an act of merit. It's what we do
When we don't possess enough information to be
Certain. It should be tentative and honest:
"This is what I think, but I could be wrong."
And what of the sophisticates?
The Jews and Christians, perhaps the
Occasional Muslim, who don't believe
Every word is perfect and from God,
Who screw up their faces at talk of Eden,
And Hell, and miracles. To you I say,
The manacles hang loose, my friends;
Slip them off and be free. And the atheists?
I'll flush the birds from the trees. You
Shoot them down if you can hit them.
That's your interest, not mine. I hope
They fly to better things.

XLII

Alpha Course

So Jesus died to save us from the Devil?
No, Jesus died to save us from God.

I thought he died to save us from evil?
No, he died to save us from good,

The radioactive goodness of a God so
'Holy' that he has to torture us for all

Eternity if we freely use our judgment
To decide what we think for ourselves.

So God killed Jesus to save us from
Our sins?

No. Men killed Jesus because they
Thought he was a troublemaker

And they were afraid he was undermining
Their authority.

So how does that translate to God punishing
Jesus for our sins?

There's no definitive answer to that question
So I'm going to do what all believers do

When asked something that exposes
Their religion. I'm going to make up

An answer that seems to fit. God
Manipulated the situation so that Jesus

Had to die and used it to punish him.
But why did he have to manipulate the

Situation? If he wanted to kill him
Why didn't he just do it? He's God after all.

I think it's because he had
To die in a dramatic way that captures

The imagination. It wouldn't have been
Much good if he'd keeled over with a pulmonary

Embolism or had a stroke, would it?
But at least it would have been God

Doing it and not men.
Also, dying on a cross is a form of torture.

The torture part is very important.
Because it's God's punishment for all our sins.

So it wasn't the death
But the torture that was key?

No: the whole shebang. Torture and
Death. The doctrine is that Jesus died

To save us from our sins.
But that of Jesus which was man would

Have died anyway. And that which was God
Could not die, at all, or it would not have been God.

It may have left His body, but it could never die.
By definition. And how exactly does this

Take our sins from us? Aren't we still as
Responsible for our actions as we ever were?

What you have to understand is that it doesn't have to
Make any kind of sense. It's a mystery.

And we're all saved. All of us?
No, only those who believe all of this.

The rest must go to Hell forever for being
Such ungrateful little bastards.

But that's the majority of the people
Who have ever lived, isn't it?

Straight is the gate, and narrow is the way.
You mean that, after all that, God was a failure?

XLIII

Want to Believe

"You believe what you want
To believe. I'll believe what
I want to believe."
There, in a phrase, is the
Dishonesty of your religion.
You believe what you want
To believe. I'll follow
The evidence.

XLIV

Flying

Reason and imagination,
Two wings of the mind.
The hide-and-seek God
Hacks off reason and gives
The bleeding bird to his
Squabbling prophets, who
Fling it off the edge of a cliff.
"I'm flying!" cries the believer,
As he plunges to the rocks below.
"I'm flying!"

XLV

mohammed is irrelevant, and jesus is irrelevant,
and moses is irrelevant, and whether you drink
is irrelevant, and what you wear is irrelevant, and
what you eat is irrelevant, and fasting is irrelevant,
and the 'virgin' birth is irrelevant, and the shahada
is irrelevant, and the nicene is irrelevant, and holy
books are irrelevant, and propaganda buildings are
irrelevant, and the call to prayer is irrelevant, and
the jealous god is irrelevant, and prophets are
irrelevant, and the male god is irrelevant, and
sharia is irrelevant, and all legalism is irrelevant,
and the crucifixion is irrelevant, and angels are
irrelevant, and demons are irrelevant, and the trinity
is irrelevant, and the demand for belief is irrelevant,
and hell is irrelevant, and heaven is irrelevant, and
the sabbath is irrelevant, and the haj is irrelevant.
only the man or woman standing before you and the way
you treat them, only that is relevant.

XLVI

"how dare you
question god?"
"i'm not. i'm
questioning man.
god can chip in
any time he likes."

XLVII

"Because I said so": a rotten
Argument even for God. Is it possible
Men possess better intellect?
Are the reasons of God so unsound
He fears scrutiny? "Behold the beauty
And elegance of my thought."
But I am not tongue-tied in the face
Of the children of Abraham.
"Blasphemy," they scream. "How dare
You insult our prophet?" "Who are
You to say such things?" Distraction
Indignation of the lie discovered.
When the cracks show, plug them
With spittle and blood. "Thou shalt
Not put the Lord thy God to the test."
So convenient. The only way to
Discover if it *is* the Lord thy God
Forbidden.

He can do whatever He wants, can't He?
What's the point of being God, otherwise?
Power, power, power, they obsess like nerdy kids
Scoring points for favourite superheroes.
There are many things a man can do
But won't: steal from old ladies, torture

Kittens, go to the local primary school with
A machete. Yes, yes, some do, but
They're less than the rest of us, not more.
And we recognise, all of us, a progression
Of rationality that puts a gorilla that
Could kill a man with bare hands below that
Same man, with his rational mind.
Reason takes precedence over mere
Capricious will.

Satan omnipotent is no justification for
Worshipping Satan. And beyond a certain
Point quantity of power makes no difference.
He could do whatever he wants and you'd
Submit to His will or suffer the consequences.
"Torture babies, for that is my will." Fuck off,
For that is mine. You see Raqqa? How would
It be worse if the 'caliphate' were men of Satan?
Would it even be as brutal? Men crucified,
Thrown from buildings for being the way
God made them, beatings for clothing infractions,
Drudge women no more than slaves
Without voice or agency, a rigid, hateful, spiteful,
Joyless life, no music, no freedom of mind,
Slaughtered for the slightest independence.

God, if anything, is a God of reason.
A scientist, dealing in physics, chemistry,

Biology, maths. They're His currency.
He spends no other. There was no
Garden with magical tree and talking snake,
No Adam and Eve with incestuous children.
Darwin illuminates the darkness; the Qur'an
And Bible make it deeper. Everywhere
You've ever been or will ever go the universe
Operates on scientific principles. They bind
You together. No magician God, and you
No vague spirit wafting about. Flesh, bone,
Blood, nerves; biology governed by laws of
Physics and chemistry, governed themselves
By maths. Logic and reason at the root and
Base of all.

XLVIII

you say you have a 'relationship'
with god; you experience him
in your life. if that's true
why are you watching 'god tv'
and reading books about him?
i don't need to watch tv programmes
or read about those with whom
i have a relationship.

XLIX

Reason leads me astray
Because the mind of man
Is flawed and fallible.
So I choose revelation,
Which is infallible. There's
No confusion in revelation,
No false prophets,
No argument between religions
And within religions. It's clear
A perfect God, the foundation
Of all reality, would choose
To hide Himself and then
Send messengers to demand
Belief, even though most
People would never hear
Such a message and those
Who did would be sceptical
Because of bad experiences
With false prophets. How
Dare they ask critical questions
To try to determine true
From false. Didn't I already
Say reason is fallible? They
Should just know the truth
Of my religion magically and

Damn them to Hell if they
Doubt. Gullibility is the
Great virtue of the saved.
The gullible are guaranteed
Paradise, provided they
Happen to be born in the
Correct country that espouses
The correct doctrines. It's no
Accident the average IQ
In Hell is Higher than
In Heaven. Just sign the dotted
Line; don't worry about small print.
Do as I say because I know
Better than you. And if you refuse
Remember God is Love.
Tough love.

L

Let's at least call Him
The Hell God that He is,
Conjured from the lower
Depths of human inspiration,
Laden with human prejudice
And cruelty, tribal bias, and
Sprinkled with hundreds and
Thousands to call it cake.

And when this vile human
Construct from a primitive age
Lies burning in the street
I'll saunter past with full bladder
And a grin on my face, and
I'll thank the Mother of all
Things for a new and better age.

LI

That God who permits hunger, cold and pain
Here would never allow it in paradise, where
He's also master! Except He's proved He's
Precisely the sort of God who does allow such things.

And that same God who swears He'll inflict
Unending agony on the majority of people
Who've ever lived – this is the God you're relying
On for eternal bliss?

LII

Jephtha's Daughter

*Men never do evil so fully and so happily
as when they do it for conscience's sake.*
                                        Pascal

And Jephthah vowed a vow unto the Lord, and said, If thou shalt without fail deliver the children of Ammon into mine hands, Then it shall be, that whatsoever cometh forth of the doors of my house to meet me, when I return in peace from the children of Ammon, shall surely be the Lord's, and I will offer it up for a burnt offering.
          The Book of Judges 11:30–31

  That was when I first thought
  You were disgusting. Long ago,
  Before belief became full blown.
  Before the holy cataracts ripened.

  The honouring of the murder vow
  More sacred than innocent life.
  Indifference who should come from
  That door till it's someone he cares
  For, emblematic of all those things
  Believers do with such serene certainty.

  Doubt doesn't fly planes
  Into buildings.
  Doubt doesn't throw men
  From roofs because of
  The way You made them.
  Doubt doesn't burn
  'Witches' and 'heretics'.

Doubt doesn't murder
Apostates.
Doubt doesn't give away
Other people's countries
And command their children's
Slaughter.
Doubt doesn't grovel
Before a Hell God.

Faith detonates mountains;
Doubt checks to see
Who lives there.
Faith justifies anything
With the words "I believe".
Doubt wants to hear more.

Men yearn for certainty, but
If God wished us to be certain
It would be the work of
An instant to prove Himself
Beyond all doubt.

LIII

Let My People Go

moses jones, no one special,

just another man in heaven,
soaked in bliss like ignorance,
chasing a ball that's flown too far,
dares to peer around the rim,
the forbidden perimeter, down
at the molten seething mass below.

billions tortured, screaming,
by the gentle smiling god who
cannot do enough for moses'
happiness. how long had it been
since that day of great division?
a million years? more?

time flies when you're having fun.
but now he remembers.

remembers the family and friends,
the good men and women condemned
who, to his shame, he's forgotten.

"they deserved it," he whispers.
then catches sight of an old
neighbour, a doctor, who'd
saved many lives, a man of
quiet dignity. they look at each
other and the old man shudders
and screams as heat melts his limbs,

which grow again, fresh and healthy
for new sadistic agony unending.

"how can this be?" says moses to
himself. "is God so full of hate and
spite to do such things?"

an angel hears and warns:
"careful friend, to ask such
questions is to beg to join him.
enjoy your place in paradise, and
keep your mouth and mind shut."

moses pulls back from the precipice,
returns to his friends, but no longer
wants to play ball. no longer wants
to do anything. his pleasures turn
to ashes in his mouth.

"most of us below in that terrible
pit," he says to himself,
"and I sing praises to the one who
keeps them there."

just then he spies a former nazi,
murderer of countless jews,
gypsies, homosexuals, communists,
anyone he happened to hate.

"what's he doing here?" he asks himself,
but knows the answer. the man,
in his last moments, had converted to
true religion and would live in paradise
for all eternity. he thinks of the doctor
melting in the flames below and feels sick.

"i must do something but i'm scared."

looking around he sees the angel:
"i need an audience with god," he says.

the angel breathes deep and shakes
his head, disappointed. "he's expecting
you," he replies.

"well?" says god.

moses quakes but it's too late.
the thought of the doctor drives him on.

"my god, i have to ask you. let my
people go that they may be free from
the hand of evil."

"and if I refuse?" wonders god.
"will you send a plague of locusts?"

"i'll do the only thing I can do. see you
as you are. a god who forms a universe,
then waits nearly fourteen billion years to
create human kind, but after as little as fifteen
or twenty years of individual life, at most a
hundred, impatient to condemn to hell forever.
a god, the foundation of all reality, who
hides himself, then sends messengers to demand
belief, a god who condemns those who follow
false prophets but reviles those who insist
on thinking for themselves to sift out the
liars, a god able to speak to the whole of
humanity in an instant so there could be no
doubt but reveals himself in such a way
that no religion of revelation is free from
dispute and division, a god who makes us
so the highest part of our humanity is
reason, but expects us to abandon it for
blind and gaping faith, a god who makes
life a test of doctrines to assent to instead
of kindnesses accumulated in layers and the loves
and stories of our hearts, a narrow-minded, petty,
vengeful god. who would worship a god like you
if they weren't afraid? what sort of god approaches
his creation through fear?"

"finished?" asks god.

"not quite. when i leave here i'll gather all the people and we'll demand a new dispensation without cruelty or torture. if you refuse we'll join our brethren below and you'll be nothing but a devil torturing the whole of mankind, pointless and vindictive."

"i could stop you."

"you could, but then you and i would both know you're afraid of one man and his words."

LIV

They Even Stole the Sun

a bit of luck really,
to be born with that
lump of gristle between
my legs, and those
tender, longing balls.
the badge of god's
approval, the seal
of superiority!

with a cock you can
strut around and never
have to think about
hoovering or washing
up or cleaning skid
marks from pants.
instead you get
interesting, important
stuff. it's god's will.

in the beginning
he was tribal, fierce,
savage. that jealous
thug of a male deity mixed
like poison in a cup of nectar,
by some long forgotten
genius, with the infinite.
a tainted source that led
to the three-headed monster
that bestrides the world even
today.

and what became of this
male god's wife? did he beat
her, perhaps, to death?
she must have existed too.
a male is to impregnate
a female; without female

is irrelevant, pointless,
impotent, a blind alley.
it nowhere exists. to give
birth to the universe is a
female endeavour, the
defining act of god.

*"there is no division in
god!"* so *"he"* is a blasphemy
as masculinity puts it there.

and that old man upstairs,
the god of 'abraham, isaac,
and jacob', defined by the
males he's god of,

that old god and his
frat-house prophets, priests,
popes, rabbis, imams,

half the human
race attuned to the divine
frequency by that special
antenna. the other half unclean
by discharge of blood.

ever doubt it's a male god
they worship these frat boys?

'lord', 'father', 'son', 'master',
'he', 'allah'. it's a male
god sending male prophets
with a message for men
to control his celestial glass
ceiling.

"god is not male,
god is spirit. it's just a way
of speaking!"

great! then from now on we say
"mother", "lady", "she", "daughter".
it makes more sense, anyway,
the longing to nurture, birthing
the universe. but look how it

changes

everything,

and those holy books
written by men, what would they
be if the divine mother were
their author? how would history
have altered had the female
potential been unchained?

"but we have a woman priest"

bully for you! belatedly some of you
have women priests and rabbis,
but look at the fuss, and only
as a result of an intellectual
milieu hostile to your beliefs, a
true enlightenment.

*"they wouldn't have received
messages from a woman prophet."*

is that so? the infinitely powerful
god constrained by what men
would receive? the message
tailored to what men would deign
to hear? the revelation of *truth*?

if you insist "god is spirit, not male",
you won't have any trouble
crying with me: "fuck the father! fuck
the male god! fuck him!"

i pin that old god down
by his cock. i drive
a nail through it.
i stand back and mock
as he squeals and writhes.

that's for jephtha's daughter,
that's for hypatia, and
that for asma bint marwan.
the hammer beats out
the rhythm of a new
freedom. i dance
for joy and venerate
she who gave birth
to everything.

PART III

THE MOST HATED MAN IN THE WORLD

Blame

Lord of the mob,
He fears no man.
But all men fear his fame.

All avoid his gaze, and flee
His presence. All
Tremble at his name.

He is king killer,
Vanquisher of generals,
He disseminates as flame.

And though they writhe
And protest at his
Indignation's shame,

There are no ears to
Hear them. All excuses
Meet disdain.

a place to go mad in

it is the light that must be blamed,
and blame it i do. i accuse and hurl
stones. rocks i aim for its head.
light that wakes from slumber, from
a place of no wounds, a place of
no trembling, a place of no tears.
look what i have to show it boasts,
but did i ask to see? now formed
i must be torn apart, now flesh i
must rot. i am a victim of light.
we are victims together. worship
the light, the light that burns! or
you will go to a hot and bright place,
full of light. light so bright it dazzles
and blinds. it is darkness to
fragile eyes. it crucifies the nerves.
it is violent, like sun,
it is cruel and there is no rest in it,
it is hate and there is no shade in it.
no breeze for your face, no escape
from the light. it is a place to go
mad in. and, given time, all men do.

Daddy

why bother with a god content to watch six million die
without lifting a metaphysical finger? are there no
bulrushes by the rhine? why not pester the abomination
with mosquitoes and frogs? or customise the angel of
death with zyklon b to fumigate the aryan first-born?
it worked once, why not again? did he not see the affliction
of his people? did he not hear their cry by reason of
their taskmasters? did he not know their sorrows?
why even wait for the murder to start? "get out now!
in a decade that lunatic will slaughter you all."
what are we to conclude when omnipotence and
omniscience collude?

knew it was going to happen

        could have stopped it

didn't

what did you do in the war, Daddy?
i hear the fatuous talk about miracles. god
intervening in lives in some coincidental way,
and it makes me sick. their self-importance makes
me sick. i have no time for a partial god who chooses
a minuscule fraction of the human race to be 'his people'
but i have even less for a god who wilfully ignores a holocaust.

The Thief, Laughing

We catch him scrambling out the window
Swag bag bulging. You might expect contrition,
Or at least acknowledgement, but he knows
Us too well. What does he do? Tosses us a
Few of our own trinkets, winks slyly, and puts
A finger to his lips. One of us starts to
Protest. "Thief!" he yells. The thief nods,
Subtle, hardly troubling, a slight raising of
The head in the direction of the troublemaker.
The mob descends on him as the thief,
Laughing, continues on his way.

The Process That I Am

Life is a biological process,
Which is a form of chemistry.
We don't say, when other
Processes come to an end,
That there is a hidden, secret,
Part of them that survives. We
Don't say it of other forms,
Amoebas or chimps.
Only we are privileged. The
Difference between me and
A chimp 1.92% DNA. Is
This where the soul is hidden?

A Revelation

Insanity is the defeat of reason.
Revealed religion is the defeat
Of reason. For both it doesn't
Matter what you say: they'll find
A way to believe.

Foundation of a Civilisation

"The accused is charged
With murder. You're his counsel?"

"No, Your Honour. I'm here because
The law demands that someone pay
For this heinous crime. So I'm offering
Myself in his place.
Punish me instead."

"Did you do it?"

"No. The accused did it.
But justice demands someone
Is punished."

"Then why shouldn't I punish
The accused?"

"As long as someone is punished,
What does it matter?"

Just the Facts

Here's what they say:
"You're going to die.
But if you believe
A certain set of
Doctrines a part of
You we call the 'soul'
Will survive forever,
In bliss, in a place
We call 'heaven'.
There may be singing.
But if you find all
Of this ridiculous
And refuse to delude
Yourself into believing
What you don't believe
Then you will be made
To suffer eternally.
It is God's justice."
Now the facts:
"You're going to die.
Your body will rot.
This may or may not

Be the end of your
Existence. It would
Appear to be, but
Nobody knows for
Certain. If they did,
They would have
Knowledge instead
Of faith. This is all
We can say for sure,
And anyone who says
Otherwise is lying."

Why Things Are Shit

It can't be God
So it must be us.
Not so much us
As them. Women.
Before that it was
Perfect. What did
They do? Disobeyed
God, of course.
It's just logic,
Really.

Divine the Right

What right have you to rule?
The democrats present
Their arguments and let you choose.

What right have you to rule?
The tyrants brandish guns
And smile.

Putin's Mother

She stares transfixed,
Lost in wonder.
Eyes stare back
So blue. They seem
To know her. If, even
Now, less than an hour
After He came from
Within her body, she
Could see the bullet-
Riddled corpse of
Anna Politkovskaya,
If she could see the
Bodies, piled in heaps,
Of her son's victims,
Would she smother
Him in her arms?
If she's not worthless
Herself, she would.

My Country Right or Wrong

"Through the sewer; there's
No other choice."

I set off in another direction and as
They wade through the shit

I hear them cursing: "He can't
Be trusted. He's a traitor."

Love Poem

He would die for her yes.
The heat of their youth a catalyst
For a process unsung, unstaged,
Unrhymed. Her corns, the flabby
Cheeks of her arse, her watery
Eyes, parts of the sacredness
Of her. She is a fragile thing,
Struggling now. And he contemplates
With sadness, and regrets
The many times he caused her
Pain. And his love is mingled
With pity, and he would die for her.

eggs in moonshine

"why do you swim so hard
against the torrent? where
are you going?"

"to the palace
beyond the clouds."

"how do you know
of this palace?"

"our belief holds it
in the sky."

"what would happen
if you stopped believing?"

"it would fall."

Fear teaches me
I want to live,
But blinds me
To how.

The End of War

The war to end all wars,
They say. And that's what
Makes it worth the while.
Consign it to the dust heap
With the perfectibility of man.
Hate metastasises, and the
Doctors waste of the same
Disease. "Never again," we
Swear, so solemn, straight-
Faced even.

But only one war will end
Them all. And that is the war
That wipes us, like a cure,
From this planet's face.
And even then, when our nearest
Relatives rise, do you think
They will achieve what we
Never could?

The Rose Centre 18.10.17

Here we are again, to see
If that pig has scratched
His dirty fingernail in your
Flesh. I would beg but
I know what he does to kids,
To babies. "Mercy!" I'd drop
To my knees, but see only
Gristle where ears should be.

"How are you? Feeling a bit
Wobbly?" says a nurse to
A woman in tears, arm on her
Shoulder.

I look around at those ahead
Of me in the queue, though I
Don't know it for sure. My
Name could be first. I watch
Him, anxious to see if he looks
At you. Or me. "It'll be fine,"
We tell each other as he
Licks the face of a girl sitting
Petrified with her parents,
And gropes under her shirt.

The Naming of the Animals

And out of the ground the Lord
God formed every beast of the field,
And every fowl of the air; and brought
Them unto Adam to see what he would
Call them. "I'll call this one Dodo,"
Said Adam and hacked off its head.
"And this is the Great Auk." Casually
He stamped on its spine and a
Satisfied smirk spread across his
Face. "Javan Tiger!" he grinned
Blowing out its brains. "Tasmanian
Tiger!" as a second round clattered
To the ground. "Woolly Mammoth!"
He whooped, hurling a spear to
Its neck. "Black Rhino, Irish Elk,
Ground Sloth, Barbary Lion, Warrah!"
Throwing back his head in manic glee
He let rip with an Uzi. "What's with all
The forests?! They spoil my view!"
He shrieked and brandished a chainsaw.

Finally, panting, a bleeding Cebu warty
Pig screaming at his feet, a laughing
Owl tumbling from the sky, he popped
In some gum, slung his gun over his
Shoulder, and turning to his appalled maker
Raised an unimpressed eyebrow.
"So, what else d'ya got?"

Time-Honoured Tactic

The other day I landed
On a God channel and
Watched in appalled
Fascination. The speaker
Disparaged the Pharisees
And Sadducees for being
Men of learning. He glorified
Instead ignorance. It's the
Time-honoured tactic of
The Abrahamic myth.

Don't ask questions,
Don't think, deny the very
Part that separates you
From dumb beasts.
He spoke of a dream an
Associate had, a dream
From God. If God is going
To speak then why not just
Speak? Why all this infantile
Hide and seek? "Guess where
I am. Is this Me or are you

Deluding yourself?"
Grow up!

Vague prophecies, wishful
Thinking and excitable halfwits
Are too tiresome and not worth
My time.

I haven't forgotten the 'Miracle
Of the Neck', that pivotal
Moment when God suspended
The laws of nature just for your
Aching muscles, though bullets
Still ripped through the hearts
Of children and mouths went
Unfed. I note, by the way, that
Dad still has Alzheimer's.
If your God is so keen to heal,
If your God is so 'great', then let
Him heal that. Ah, but God won't
Be tested, will He? How very
Convenient.

The point, however, isn't to test
What God can do. The point
Is to test whether it's God at all.

But that's not the game, is it?
Guess and be certain, and if you
Guess wrong it's off to the incinerator
With you.

It's sly, and cruel, and absurd.
Don't test God, but the truth
Can always be tested. That is
How we distinguish it from
The lie. Only now we're supposed
To rely on dreams and conjecture
And preposterous claims that don't
Withstand scrutiny. But that's ok,
Because you'd only scrutinise if you
Doubted, and doubt is a sin.

Hide and Seek

"Come on, it'll be fun!" he says.
"I don't want to. Go and play
With someone else."
"Who'd you have in mind?"
Some names occur: Putin,
Mugabe, Erdogan, Kim Jong-un,
But he's already on the move.
"Here I go. No peeking."
He grins, and before I say another
Word he skips off, laughing,
Light on his toes for such
A big fellow. And so the game begins.
As dull and terrifying as it's been
Since the first amoeba learned
The rules.

You heard me.

You don't need brains for this.
Even idiots can play. In fact,
They always do.

One, once the game begins each
Contestant is in play at all times,
In all places, no matter what they're
Doing or who they're with.
Two, the decision of your opponent
Is final. Three, your opponent can
Do anything he wants. Anything.
He can't cheat 'cos he's not
Bound by rules. But you are.
Four, you lose. Winning is simply
Postponing losing as long as you can.

You feel him breathing down
Your neck. He likes to disguise himself:
A snake, a spider, a rusty nail,
A bullet, a bomb. You're driving
Happily along and he strokes the
Brain of the man coming towards you.
But sometimes too it's fun to string it out.
Jumping from behind a lamp post and
Screaming at the top of his voice so your
Heart seizes. Then he leaves you
For another day. Modern medicine
His foreplay.

He can be anywhere. The pavement,
A grand piano above your head,
A loose nut, or a nut on the loose,
The prick of a rose, fur in your arteries,
A virus or an asteroid a million miles from
Earth. Tell yourself that there's another world
Where he can't play if you like, where life
Is not biological. But in the meantime
He's out there, sniggering into his hand.
I hate this game. So do you.
Now play.

Ad Hoc Architects

Ad hoc architects, we're so grateful
When the self settles. Floorboards
Squeak, the roof leaks and protests
In the wind. Keep your fingers crossed

Against subsidence, or worse.
Some collapse completely, burn
To the ground, exposed wires, leaking gas,
Or maybe the wolf huffs and puffs.

At any rate, why disturb things and
Take a risk? The self is settled, the
House is warm and relatively comfortable,
Who cares if a few rats scuttle across the carpet

And roaches share your food? Is this
Why we hate those who disagree and ask
Questions? Tremors in reality threatening
To bring the whole thing crashing down.

And what then? The slow construction
Of a new self? What if you're sixty,
Seventy, eighty? Your whole life a lie?
It's like living in a tent at the bottom of the garden

For your last few years. Is honesty worth that?
But, if denial is to be the criterion by which we live,
We may as well find the most self-serving delusion
In which to cower. It's where we'll spend our lives.

A Few Thoughts on the Death of Anne Boleyn

Think of Anne Boleyn. Tried, sentenced,
Grovelling in her cell at prayer.
Do you suppose she begged the God
She served with such fervour: "Please
Don't let them do this. You know I'm
Innocent." How could she not?
And what reply could she receive
But the silence of the stones?

Could anyone have saved her?
Could the guard have said,
"I'm not bringing her to the
Scaffold. She's just a young
Woman. Killing her is senseless"?

Could the axe man have said,
"Let's reorder society so that
People don't die at the whim
Of a solitary man"?

Could the crowd have demanded,
"It's our will that you let her live.

We are the people. We
Are sovereign!"?

Could the courtiers have argued,
"Even if the accusations are true,
Henry, this is too brutal and
Merciless, and it's really just an
Excuse so you can marry Jane
Seymour"?

Could even the King have spared
Her? As brittle as all tyrants are,
As reliant on fear, how long would
He have survived if he'd shown
Compassion to the mother
Of his child?

What if no one in the world
Had wanted her to die?
If everyone wanted her to live
Who could intervene? But the
World doesn't work like that.
We are set in social concrete
Only heat can melt. And, though
In molten form it changes shape,
You'd better be quick. It soon
Sets hard again, as solid as before.

Things We Say

All the things we say
About God with such
Certainty.
"What is God?"
"Spirit."
Who knows what that is,
Or if it even exists?
What we mean is God is
Not matter, the same stuff
As you, as me, as slime.
Matter that's alive is biological
And can be killed. Unless it's
Some form of 'divine matter',
Like an immortal rock or gas.
In any case, hardly transcendent,
And theologians teach that God
Is perfect.

Another thing we say is that God
Is omnipresent. But no one likes
To dwell on actual implications.
Is God present in that foul-

Smelling dog turd?
"Oh, if you're going to be silly…"
But that's the thing. I'm in earnest.
It's the doctrine. And if you don't
Think it through you're just ignoring
Inconvenient questions that lead
To the actual.

We talk of omniscient God designing
The universe, but could it be otherwise?
All intelligence that we've encountered
Is just another evolved response to
Environmental forces, like echo-location,
Or the ability to swim or speak. Maybe
When we say "God", what we're referring
To is a transcendental moulding force, like
The Big Bang, Evolution, the way a
Glacier makes a valley.

And, on the subject of the Big Bang,
Of creation, how about the notion
That God is 'outside time'? Another
Doctrine to dodge an obvious problem.
What is subject to time begins and ends
And can change for the worse. You can
See how theologians might not be keen.

But it doesn't follow it's necessarily so.
The problem is this: that which is
Outside time can't do anything, can
Have no agency. To create is to change.
That which is created did not exist; now
It does. The creator was not a creator;
Now He is. If I make a vase I must
Use the operation of time. I do. I make.
To do is to act in time. There's no
Timeless doing. It is not nothing
Creating a Universe. God does, God
Makes. It's what makes God God
(Or not, but that's another question…).
If He does then He becomes what
He was not, and is, by this process,
Temporal.

prodigal

yeah, you do that, kill the fatted calf,
but when we all calm down from our great
joy, what then?

does what's left go to both of us
now he's back?
if so I'm the one who's
bankrolled the waster.

tell me, how's that fair?
why should the rest of my life
be poorer and harder because
he wanted to go out and piss it

all away on girls and wine?
i don't know what to make
of your reaction, except maybe
he's your favourite and you
don't care that you're doing me

an injustice.

Cup of Poison

"And when the Lord thy God shall deliver them before thee; though shalt smite them, and utterly destroy them; thou shalt make no covenant with them, nor shew mercy unto them."

Deuteronomy 7:2

"The solution to the Middle East is in the Bible. The land was given to Israel"
Jewish settler woman

the solution, if there is one, must be based on rational principles,
not a book of nonsense about a spiteful, partial, hateful god.

the jewish people are nothing special. they're not chosen. there's no
international jewish conspiracy. they're just men and women like everyone else.

no better, no worse than you. or me.

call me an anti-semite, it's just a propaganda smear. long live the jewish people.
long live israel! but death to their false god and his lies.

why would god choose the descendants of abram as his holy people when they
so frequently rejected him?

haven't there been, throughout the ages, many of different faiths
willing to give everything for god, even if convinced by different doctrines?

did god not understand

they too were seeking him with all their hearts and minds?
so why not honour their children with the title 'chosen'?

the truth is, yahweh is just a tribal god elevated above his station
unfit to wield the power foisted upon him. and like all things tribal he's divisive.

i am as much a child of the creator as the jew, the muslim, the christian, the
pagan. my life held in being each moment by the same divine will.

no fit parent plays favourites. and what is god if not the parent of our kind?
it's fatuous to try to win the argument by saying "god is on my side", and unprovable.

if god wants to give a chunk of land to one nation and evict another let him
appear to all of us and make it clear. no need then for the slaughter of children,
the evicted can pack their bags and make their exodus,

and make their own minds up about the god who takes sides. the problem with
'holy' books isn't the vile verses. it's the good and inspiring ones that make us
blind to them, or excuse them.

we must remember always that a cup of water with a few drops of poison
is a cup of poison.

Always

And God said, "I have tested the human race
Too hard. I overestimated their capacity for love."
And He removed race and religion and poverty
From the world.

But wars still raged across the face of the Earth,
For hate will find a way.

"Pesky humans!" said God. And all gold and silver
And platinum, and every jewel of any description
Was removed from the world. "And I'd better do
Oil while I'm at it," mused God. And He surveyed
His work and saw that it was good.

But wars still raged across the face of the Earth,
For hate will find a way.

"I should have gone with my gut instinct
And created a hermaphrodite race," sighed God.
And male and female: He uncreated them.
"That should fix it. What could they possibly
Fight about now?" And He prepared for a well earned

Night in front of the telly with a G&T and some nibbles.

BANG! The rockets flew.
CRACK! Bullets bit into human flesh.

"Land! I forgot land!" God cried, slapping his head.
And changed the laws of the universe so that
Only unowned land could be productive or
Profitable in any way. "Surely even the human race
Can't find a pretext for war now."

But right-handers killed left-handers, and brown-
Eyed killed blue-eyed, and the tall killed the short.
For hate will find a way in the heart of men

Always.

The Glory of the World

God confronted Satan with His chef-d'oeuvre,
"What do you think of this?" he asked, puffing out
His chest with pride. "I've set mankind over all
Creation!"

Satan squinted across the distances of space,
Across the galaxies he peered. Perplexed,
Apologetic, he turned to God and shrugged.
"I don't see them," he admitted.

"On that rocky planet, there. Follow my finger."
"I still don't… Oh, you mean those two apes?
On that tiny speck? In the middle of nowhere?"

"Er… yeah. That's them. Aren't they fabulous?"
But suddenly God seemed less cocksure.

"They're rather good!" replied the angel,
Trying to sound convinced.

"Be honest," said God.

A weary expression crossed the seraph's face.
"Lord, I've traversed the entirety of the universe,
Visited every planet, holidayed in event
Horizons, debated with species far
Superior to human beings. I'm an immortal.
So how exactly is mankind the Lord of Creation?"

"Hah!" laughed God, reddening. "Got me there!
Pity, though. I had this amusing idea you might spend
Your every waking moment plotting mankind's downfall by
Making them eat an apple, and then I was going to turn you
Into a snake. And then you'd be the arch-enemy of the
Human race until the end of time, when I'd hurl you into a
burning pit… We could still do it, if you like?"

Satan suppressed a groan. "A species that limited
Would never believe cosmic forces were fighting
Over them. And what does it matter to me if they eat an apple
Or lord it over their tiny world? They're so dim
They'll probably ruin it in a few millennia anyway."

God looked crestfallen. "You know something,
Satan? I have way too much time on my hands."

fair to the clerics

i accept you were genuinely looking
for me, and a rose is a rose, and all that.
and the reason you chose as you did is
because certain ideas seemed improbable
and others more likely, and i suppose you'll
feel hard done by when i burn you. but if i
just let anyone in whose heart is in the right
place what would my clerics police? it wouldn't
be fair to tread on their toes.

i am a secret self,
unknown even to myself,
though guessed at
and wished at and
hoped at. i see things
i wish to see, remember
a different life of better
deeds and dubious
justifications fortified
by half-closed eyes,
past generated by present,
creature of my imagination.
i present as partial truth, a
different me for different
friends, a separate self to
each. or is it that i contain
multitudes? i know things
in me that they do not, and
equally am seen with other
eyes that delve where i
disdain to see. even honesty
muddles me, muddies me
as silt disturbed in water.
how can i ever tell if truth
i try to tell myself is true
or not? i am a secret self,
unknown even to himself,
who wishes he were not.

Older

As I grow older I find myself
More and more prone to emotion.
I've always hated glib sentimentality,
But now a song, a name, some
Sudden remembrance or notion

And my voice wavers, my eyes
Well. Anger and sadness seem
To be the main culprits. Anger at
Human stupidity, and sadness that
My world, everything I have seen,

Loved, or will ever love, is going to
Disappear. So much already gone,
The world of my youth a fading memory.
And now, in my early fifties, I understand
How easy it is to end one's days alone.

The great rocks of my childhood are crumbling.
The great losses of my life are looming.
My infancy, a joy for my father and mother:
Birth, growth, energy. Their childhood
A sorrow to me. A list of ailments dooming

Them to indignity and death. Dementia,
Diabetes, atrial fibrillation, arthritis, a green-
House of anxiety and depression. And I have
My doubts that age has brought me wisdom.
Though I embrace the Stoics I am not serene,

I've forgotten as much as I've learned, and I've
Never been a patient man. But perhaps
The reason for my increased sensitivity is that I see
The fragility of all things. Perhaps the sadness,
Even anger, is because the inescapable traps

That lie in wait arouse in me compassion.
Isn't that the real lesson of age?
I look at a man like Trump, so devoid
Of empathy, a failure as a human
Being, who appeals only to prejudice and rage,

And mixed with my contempt I find at times
For him too something akin to pity.
Incapable of seeing this great lesson
That life is trying to teach him. Strutting around,
A grizzling pouting child, a sociopathic Walter Mitty.

The Great Flood

God's older brother popped his head around the bathroom door:
"Hey, Yahweh, you're slopping water everywhere, what're
You doing?" The young deity looked up startled and replied:
"Drowning the human race. They're so evil." And he watched
Fascinated as an elderly man gasped and floundered, searching
For a foothold in the depths. "You're such a little psychopath!"
Said the brother. "What about the millions of children? And
If you think they're all so bad, why don't you make a new species
That's better?" God fished the old man from the water and laid him
Gently on the bathmat. Grinning he took out a magnifying glass
And, catching the sun through the window, fried the old fellow
To a crisp. "I like them just the way they are," he said.

In the Dark

On the sea in the dark of night
The bay lights sparkled. A single
Gleam cried: "It's all about me. I'm
The most important." Then
Disappeared from sight.

holy words

these are my holy words:
"no", "why?", "fuck you",
"i disagree", "i have as much
right to speak as you", "that
can't be right", "you haven't
thought it through", "you're
no one special", "you're just
a servant of the people, not
our master", "no one is
above the law", "you haven't
answered my question",
"i have a right to know what
you do in my name", "from
where do you get your
legitimacy?", "resist a tyrant
to the death!"

unholy word

i'll tell you a dirty word
doctrine
it is the filthiest of words
men have died for it
killed for it
it is the corruptor of minds
it is perversion
once exposed men crucify
will burn and rack and rape
will call the psychopath's trade
'goodness' and kindness 'evil'
those who question are suspect
are witches saving their own
it is a screaming word a panic
word
it is closed and small and blind
counting millimetres
fearing laughter as
death fears life
pompous
self-righteous

smug
it is a word you must obey
it has no syllable of mercy
and declines always to death

wanna set the world
on fire? words are
matches. but have
a care, my friend.
not all is tinder,
and a fire once set
goes where it will.

In Spades

I am an equal opportunities hater.
I don't give a fig about your race,
Your colour, your gender.

Call me a race traitor, why don't
You? You wouldn't be wrong.
It matters nothing to me

If I'm the last 'white' man
On Earth, though as a matter
Of fact I'm a sort of pinky orange.

I've yet to meet someone truly
'White'. So much bullshit is
Spoken about race:

Black vs White, all so easy,
So lazy, so black and white.
But though I've known many

People with rich and beautiful
Brown skins not one so far
Has been actually black.

Maybe I don't get out much. In any
Case, what you are left with
If you take away my race

Is the same. People. A human
Race of constant squabbles,
Doctrines, wars, destruction

Of other species and complete
Stupidity, the grand constant
Of history, spread evenly,

Fairly, throughout our kind.
And so the forests disappear,
Land labelled 'unused' ready

For a good concreting, extermination
Of one species after another
Until we walk our barren Earth

And see that it is good. Only
It won't be. What it will be,
In spades, is what we deserve.

jesuitical

swallow the lie
while you are fry
the hook stays
in you till you die

The Human Duty

The dead don't care
About justice.
The murdered man doesn't
Know he ever existed.
His blood is silent,
Crying for nothing,
Soaked in dirt.
He feels no anger,
No offence.
The outrage of a moment
Before wiped clean.

The universe does not care
About justice.
It doesn't know the murdered
Man ever existed.
It doesn't know the
Murdering man prospers,
And it does not care.

The universe does not
Punish evil or reward good.
The universe is rocks and
Water and light and dark
And wood and elements
And fungi and bats and whales
And stars and gas.
It is a jumble of things
That do not care
For the murdered man
Or the man who murdered him.

But you care about justice.
You know the murdered
Man existed and you must see
That the murdering man
Does not prosper.
It is a human duty alone
And if you will not do it
It will not be done.
And there will be no justice.

On Their Way

Sometimes I remember
Those thugs are on their
Way and I can't think about
Anything else. What's the
Point of arctic roll, vodka
And tonic, reading,
Learning Greek? What's
The point of anything
At all? Soon they'll be
Here, kneecapping, glee
Clapping, eye prodding,
Nerve shredding, bone
Scrapping. They'll tear
The hair from my scalp,
Scrag my skin, and bleach
My eyes. A duster to the
Side of my head, and
When I'm down a bovver
Boot to make the job good.
I try on my new grin,
Toothless as an old cat,
Vacant as space.

Oh, my faithful companions,
You'll never leave me.
You don't carry your consciences
On your backs. You travel
Light, you scamps, and all
You really want is everything
I've got. Don't phone ahead.
I know you're coming. You're
Just around the corner now,
Kicking down doors in the
Next street. Yes, I could read
A book, write a letter or
Dare a peach, but you'll be here
Soon so I open the door
And cower in the corner,
Waiting, waiting, where I know
You'll be happy to find me.

Everybody Wins

Let's have a war.
It's been far too long,
Though no time at all.
Let's blow as many mothers' sons
To smithereens
As humanly possible.
Sing patriotic songs
And scream headlines
As we relish Armageddon.
Let's jeer, "That's why you're
Going down, that's why you're
Going down!" and "Who are yer?
Who are yer?" And when we've
Enjoyed our catharsis of plasma
And marrow, scattered the lands
With femurs, tibias and
Carpals eight, we can begin
The wringing of the hands.
Let's have national days
And make films, write poems
And plays. We can condemn
All war and swear to the Lord

God of Cant his sacred words:
"Never again". Historians will
Spend their days studying
"What went wrong" and "how
It happened" and we will savour
The stupidity of those who lacked
Our insight and murmur, just
Loud enough for everyone to hear:
"I was always against it."
Let's have a war! Everybody wins!
Please say we can.

Love After the Fact

"You were known and loved from
All eternity," they patter in their sales
Pitch. Read the small print.
Either God set in motion a process
Governed by accidents and
Sliding doors, and you are
Factory-hatched, not hand-
Crafted, our maker a spectator
To decisions and whims,
Events that led to you
And me, but not necessarily,
And He loves whatever drops
Onto the factory floor.
Or do you think perhaps He wanted
You in particular to love and not
Some random fluke (which
Creation rather implies, does
It not?), do you think it's all
Arranged, just so, by iron
Laws of physics and
Chemistry and the whole of
History to this point has been

Organised specifically to produce
You and no one else? Like
Designing a lawn around a
Blade of grass. More than that,
Like designing the entire history
Of a garden, past and future,
Around that blade; vaster even,
The history of the Sahara round
A single grain of sand. To get
To you decisions had to be made,
Wars won and lost, species extinct,
Nations devastated, continents
Crossed, the Holocaust, rapes
And rollercoasters, amputations
And evenings in with a bottle or two,
Goldfish in bowls or a kitten maybe,
This breakfast or that, billions murdered
At exact moments, others lovable
As you never born, the wingbeats
Of butterflies, history exact
And vast, worlds whirling with
Infinite precision, all for you, ingredients
In time's recipe that rustled up you,
So you could be known and loved,
The fulcrum of creation.

mirror mirror

all art comes from the same place
and all artists need the same implements
a shovel an unflinching eye a strong stomach
and a bloody mind

they say "tell us something pretty
tell us of clouds and flowers
tell us we'll never die"
the artist smiles and shows them
the scarred face of the child
the land mine victim hobbling on
bits of wood

the artist doesn't ignore the worm in the apple
it becomes the centre piece of his art

they say "give us only beauty"
but only beauty is a lie
and only pain is unbearable
the artist must see the world entire
unresting showing every detail
he must teach himself to see
and having done so teach others to see

they never kick the walls of reality
they just want them padded

"give us a cat" they plead
"warm and comfortable
half blind snoring on our lap"
sneezing gummy
snug with its delicate
clawless paws more like
a rug than a thing of flesh
and blood

but i give you the wolf
lean and sinew i give you
cold and hunger and pain
i give you the wilful ignorance
of men and the suffering of women

great technique
must be slave to deep vision
with grip hooks we tear the face
off reality

Having It All

There are men on mountains
And in deserts who say
To have nothing is to have
It all. They hoard their nothing
And gloat like dragons
With gold.

There are men in deserts
Who hoard their money,
And hoard their power,
And hoard their women.
They say to have everything
Is to have it all.

And there is me, lying here
With you, lost in your eyes,
Hoarding this moment.
And I say those men
Can have their nothing
And have their everything,
Because I'm the one
Who has it all.

all we have left

"air strikes, starvation,
disease. all we have left
is prayer." but you prayed
against air strikes, starvation,
disease. where did it get you?

The Knife Lies in Wait

What being stabbed in the back feels like,
But do you feel it if you don't know
It's going in? I smile in your
Face and stab from behind.
It's no super power. The knife
Hurts me too.

The smile is real and tender.
You must use the sharpest blade to have
Your cake. What would they say? The friends
Who love you more? Stupefied mouths, I hear
Them gasp: "He must be stoned!" They don't
Understand. Some things aren't looked for,

Sometimes pain blunders into your life unheralded,
Making its demands, self-entitled. Incision
The only solution, the only question where
To cut? "I shall *not* cut!" I vow.

Cowardly? Stupid? Poor fool. Think you can
Wait out your turn? Pain deals the hand, the
Players waiting. "I'll have it all. No one has
To be hurt."

Then look with surprise as blood
Drips from my hand. The knife lies in wait
Down every road, and I must wield it. Perhaps
The key is not pain but innocence. But that
Demands a stab of a different kind, full frontal,
To the death, in the heart or neck. I am not
The man for such a work.

I conjure more than one face, and on either
The trail of tears is more than I can bear.
Never plant a rose where a rose grew
Before, but sometimes the first flower is
There, blooming still and beautiful. "Is the
Garden not large enough for both?" I wonder.

Advise me, Mortimer, what has been writ?
Empower me, Janus, give me the faculty of
My sign, to live twinned lives and bring happiness
In each.

In the Beginning

What's the point of being a poet?
There's no money in it, little glory.
A few names bestride the modern world,
Heaney, Duffy, but the world is distracted
By moving pictures. Who cares for
The flotsam and jetsam of the printed
Word?

If you would be a master of men
You must be the master of words.
It is words alone can make a man
Fly a plane into a building, or jump
From it, or build it. It is only words
We fling in the face of our Great
Enemy. Only words give comfort.

A picture is worth a thousand words,
They say, but words interpret the picture.
We are a species of words, that
Link together like chains, and rope
The moon. Only words mobilise armies,
Only words march a child into a

Chamber of gas. Words alone
Have such terrible power.

Words are the masters of men,
And poets are the masters of words.
Still don't believe me?
Think of the Great War and its
Great poets. They are the interpreters
And prophets of the cataclysm.

See what you can do?
Consider the self-aggrandising
Void called Vladimir Putin, a mere
Sociopath, less than an ordinary
Man. All for the glory of Mother
Russia is all for the glory of the
Ruler of Russia.

I, mere poet that I am,
Come along like an old dog,
And cock my leg on his reputation.
With words I conjure pictures.
A custard pie in his face,
Me standing arms akimbo,
One leg on Putin's head,
A scraggy old dead lion.

And forever we shall be associated,
And he can do nothing,
For all his power and wealth.
Forever men will paint pictures
And tell jokes of me throwing that pie
In his face. Of me cocking my leg
On his great monuments. Me, mere
Scribbler of words, standing over
His body, tongue dangling to one
Side of his flatulent face, in the
Triumph of the free man.

Drowning

Love can be the hands
Of a drowning man,
Dragging you down.
"Leave him," they say.
"There's nothing you
Can do." They are
Content to watch him
Drown. The question
Is, are you?

The One Thing Heaven Can't Abide

I

Thou shalt steal from thy parents
Thou shalt eat babies alive
Thou shalt torture for pleasure
Thou shalt lie and connive
Thou shalt enslave the vagrant
Thou shalt kidnap and kill
Thou shalt rape homeless widows
Thou shalt plunder at will
Thou shalt stub out cigarettes on
The eyes of thine enemies' kids
Thou shalt consider thy duty
What the kind man forbids

II

What if the tablets of stone were
Inscribed like this? If I said "not
On your nelly!" would I be an evil man?
Does goodness shift with the divine
Whim? And if He says, "this is good
Today, evil tomorrow, and good again

The day after"? What if the Devil cried,
"Defy such commands?" Who, then,
Is my master?

III

"He'd never command
Anything like that!"
Oh, so now you speak for
God? In any case, I see
You defy the injunction to
Stupidity when it suits.
If you won't think how dare
You preach? If you will
Then why shouldn't others?
Or do you simply forbid
Different conclusions?
Prophets aren't to be
Contended with. Revelation
Must be swallowed whole;
It is not permitted to chew.

IV

God is perfect, God is perfect.
That is all our hymn.

God is perfect, God is perfect.
Obey His every whim!

V

They have it back to front!
They say, "God is perfect.
It comes from God.
Therefore it's perfect."

Assume, if you will, the
Perfection of God. If it
Comes from Him then it's
Perfect, if from men then it's
Not. So perfection is the *test*
Not the foregone conclusion.

VI

Heaven is ovine. Rejoice!
The thinking's been done for you.
The gates of Ijtihad are closed.
It doesn't matter if it's true.

VII

And what of integrity? Which
Has more? "I believe it's true.
I don't question. I simply
Accept what I'm told."
"I believe it's true. I've
Questioned deeply." Belief
Allows the unreasonable.
Reason does not.

VIII

Faith denies reason. It says,
"I am where you cannot go.
I walk on water, I fly on
Al-Buraq's back, the sun and
The moon stand still in the sky."
"Why?" I ask. "Tell me why?"

Before Him shall be gathered
All nations: and he shall separate
Them as a shepherd divideth his
Sheep from the goats. To the
Griddle with those who question
And come to their conclusions.

Those who believe without eyes
Shall inherit the kingdom prepared
For them. "Why?" I ask. "Tell
Me why?" Because God hates
Intellectuals and smart alecs.
The one thing Heaven can't abide
Is the man who thinks for himself.

IX

For all its denials faith has a dirty little
Secret. There *is* no faith without
Reason. Without it we are gibbering
Monkeys. Can one adhere to doctrines
If one has no idea what they mean?
Can one distinguish heresy? Or one
Religion from another? Those
Who would deny reason must
Appeal to its authority in their
Arguments against it. Reason
Reduces mountains to rubble,
Drills holes beneath them, flies
Above them. Faith just babbles
At the sky.

X

Every argument on its own merit.
Alcohol, pork, do this, do that.
"Because I said so" is for kids.

A minimum requirement for God
Must be superiority in reason.
Fair, then, to assume His
Commands are rational and just.
Reasonable to assume the Great
Judge won't only be fair but
Be seen to be fair, an explaining
God, not a secretive God.

"How dare you question Him!"
They snarl. The last refuge
Of the scoundrel. But they know,
And I know, and you know
They beg the question.
"Is it God or is it *man*?"
And we know the test for that.

Adventure with Foof

I can't say for sure, but it's certainly *one*
Of my earliest memories. Definitely my
First encounter with Death, though I was
Slow to realise he was being summoned.
Trotting behind Yiayia my only thought
Was to see inside the barn across the road
From her house. In my memory it looms
Like a castle for birds.

My tiny grandmother leaned over, grabbed
The portcullis by its hem and, tossing it lightly
Upwards, like a clansman with a caber,
Beckoned me inside. Clutching Foof, the
Constant companion of my little life, I hurried into
A scene of hen bedlam. Wading through
Scurrying bodies, squawking, flapping,

Histoplasmosis swirling through air,
I watched in delight as the old lady wrestled
Chickens, lunging until with triumph she
Held one aloft. And back we went, across
The street, away from our raid on the great

Castle with our captive dangling at her side,
And Foof at mine. I have no idea if I pitied
The creature but I think, in truth, any

Such feelings are retrospective. The
Chicken, without doubt, had better perspective
On what was about to occur, and I fancy
It fell silent, contemplating with terror its
Impending doom. Or perhaps the blood
Was rushing to its head. Yiayia perched on a low
Wall while I stood watching. She had a knife
And a bucket already in place and

Without a word, without warning, as though
It were the most every day mundane act,
She lifted the bird into the air by its legs
And with swift, practised movement cut off
Its head, dropping it into the bucket. I stood
Motionless, unspeaking, more astonished than
I have been since, as she tipped up the body,
Pouring out blood and ripping out innards.

And then, as the old lady serenely plucked
Feathers, some nascent moral sense awoke
Within me. I turned and ran into the house to
Find my mother, who would make it all right,
Who would apply retribution for the murdered hen.
"Mummy, mummy, Yiayia just killed a chicken,
And she meant to!" I cried. I don't remember
How she replied, though I do know the bird
Never received justice.

The limpet clings
To its little rock
For fear of the sea.
And soon conceives
Its lump of stone
Is the whole of reality.

Frustration

We were walking along
Behind two Muslim women
In traditional dress, and
I started thinking how
I distrust spirituality
That requires a uniform.
Then my thoughts turned
To doctrines and rules that
So accompany such religions
And how they entirely miss
The point. Like trying to
Translate a poem into prose.
I felt a tug on my arm:
"Did you hear what I said?"
"Sorry. I was deep in thought."
*"Your whole life you're deep
In thought. And nothing
Ever gets done!"*

a blackbird steals my
blueberries. i pick what's left
then drop some for her.

the wren fights to the
death to defend
the cuckoo in her nest

Party's Over

No one invites King Rat to the party
But he comes anyway and says it's
His party and we're his guests. We
Make to leave but King Rat says
That would be rude. King Rat doesn't
Like rudeness. Nor do his goons.
So we stay, but now no one is having
Fun, except King Rat and the rat goons.
"Why does no one smile?" asks The Rat.
"I laid on a party just for you!" Rude
Health is a contradiction in terms so
We smile and flash the teeth we'd like
To keep. "Dance!" commands The Rat.
"To my music that I provided." So we
Dance, but just the steps. As the old
Saying goes, "Who can kill the one who
Pays the piper…". The goons select who
They dance with and grin at the husbands.
Soon we're hungry so we eat his food.
It's hard to swallow but the goons gobble
It down and eat from our plates too.
"Time to leave!" scowls The Rat. "You

Guys have overstayed your welcome."
At the door the goons collect a contribution
Towards party funds. "Come and stay
At mine," I say to the former owner of the
House as The Rat fondles his daughter.

My Own Nature

If my task is to rise
Above my nature
With what but my
Nature must I
Accomplish it?
With what but my
Nature shall I be
Left when I am done?

Fixed

It's a fix, isn't it?
Projecting little lies
Into the future, hexes in cliffs.
"You'll be fine", "when you're better",
"Nothing to worry about".
Suspended, dangling between
What went before that was truly
Alive but now is dead, and what lies
Ahead, which is nothing but treachery.
Your climbing partner, look again.
Bony-fingered, fixed grin, silent.
Does he seem a mite cavalier
About health and safety? Was
That a friendly hand on your
Shoulder or was he testing your
Grip? Look down. The ground is out
Of sight. Look up. Only the clouds.
Test those hexes, make sure
They're fast. You're going to
Need them.

Cetacean Creed

Born in the Swirl and Mass,
Somehow engaged to go forward.
Move first think later. "Why am
I here?" "What is the meaning of
This?" Formulated as "What the
Hell is going on?" No! Formulated
Wordlessly. Good questions in
Any case, but darkness and teeth
Before luxury. Rule one, follow
Mother. Don't ask me how I know.
It's a cord of love and fear. And
Now we must go up and suck
At the Emptiness above. It is cold
And it fills me. I am tied to the
Emptiness more than to mother.
If I must choose I will choose
Always The Emptiness. The
Emptiness is God, where we came
From in our beginning. Where we
Go when we die. Those who enrage
It summon Demons of Emptiness,
Who wait, perched on clouds,

Shards of lightening poised to drag us
Away to a thin and desiccated place.
But The Emptiness loves us, commands
Us give thanks, sends Emissaries to
The Swirl and Mass with messages
For those who understand; the wise
Among us. Each time you go up
To the Emptiness above wonder
"Will they be there? The Emissaries,
The Demons? Is this the day I shall be
Summoned home?"

Too Dark

We clamber out of the dark and freezing ocean
And for a while huddle together in our boats.
We paddle furiously. Do we move? Beneath
Us ocean. Around us ocean. There is only
Ocean as far as the eye can see. No one
Remembers anything but the water but some
Point to the horizon:
"We have been promised land!" they cry. "Row harder!"
"Who made this promise?" I ask. "Stand up!"
"Hush!" says one. "Shame!" another.
But no one in our little flotilla stands.
Voices tell of others before, who spoke with
Authority.
"And what became of them?"
"They went into the ocean, every one."
"We must go," says the woman who pulled me
On board. She slips in with a shudder and I cry
As she disappears beneath the surface. I would
Follow but I'm afraid. I peer into the water for any
Sign of her. But it is too dark, and I see nothing.

Going up the Line

I don't want to seem
Ungrateful but I didn't ask
For any of this. I know
I'm one of the lucky ones,
You don't need to keep on.
I count my blessings daily.
But I see the casualties
Limping home and I'm
Not sure it's worth it.
If I could go back,
Fill a balance sheet before
The deal was sealed
Do you think I'd be here?
Yes, the trip through France
Was beautiful and I always
Enjoy an ocean crossing,
But it's the journey as a whole
And the destination that really
Matters. The cratered, muddy
Tracks leading on, littered with
The slaughtered and
Crippled, bleaches out the

Primary colours and memory
Fades in the face of fear.
Who, as artillery rains down,
Says to himself: "I may be blown
To smithereens or just lose a leg
But at least I've enjoyed some
Great roast dinners. I had some
Glorious sex, and first-rate
Conversations with friends."
I see them coming back.
I see the toll extracted, arthritic
Hands like claws, knees on fire,
Backs cracked and broken,
Brains wiped, mouths drooling.
I see them gasping for one more
Breath and I say, "I don't want
To go." But you signed the dotted
Line for me. And entered my name.

Still Waters

"Never" is something I've
Learned not to say.
The self is malleable
Like clay and what seems
Impossible today may be
Tomorrow's reality.

A closed mind is a
Dishonest mind, searching
For a way to resist the
Sinewy fingers of change.
"Let me never forsake you!"
I would pray.

But I was not afraid
To ask the awkward questions
Though I could see the
Answers might betray what
I stood for publicly. It's
The dismay of my tribe

Held me back for a while.
It's hard to relinquish admiration
And status within a group.
But the day came when the questions
Grew too strong, the old answers
Like a stubborn bray

And I knew I had already gone,
Pushed away into different waters.
I'm still sailing, carried by a strong
Current, and where I'll land it's difficult
To say. But I do know this: it's the
Still waters that are stagnant with decay.

The Most Hated Man in the World

A man without enemies is a shameful thing.
Kill yourself, O man. Remove yourself
From the world.

I number my enemies in billions. It is
My proudest boast. The willing slaves. The
Enemies of reason.

It is the man who tells the truth they hate.
Very well then. Let me be the most hated
Man in the world.

The Feast of Reason

What difficult questions do you ask
The one you love?

The human thing is reason but
They say roll over like a dog.

Evangelicals and mystics,
For them the shaft tipped

With the barb of mockery.
And what I find so ironic?

They must appeal to reason as final
Arbiter in the matter of its own overthrow.

A Gentle Rally

Leave your intelligence at the door:
It's not wanted here. Don't ask
Questions. Or, rather, do ask questions,
But not the deep, critical, persistent kind
That get under our skin.
We'll tell you you're stubborn and wilful.
We'll ask who you think you are.
What we want from you is inquiry:
What we say God demands of you,
What you're required to believe.
A gentle rally across a lowered net.

what happened when
slaves met free men
in the market? did they
rise up and break free
themselves? or did they
insist the free men be
enslaved as well?

Joshua Ben Joseph

God's cuckold looking mighty pissed off,
Sitting on a doorstep dragging on a
Fag. Another row with his beloved.
I sidle up, clap a hand on his shoulder,

"Come on mate, drown your sorrows."
We slope off down the Prince
For a few sneaky pints. After a couple
He opens up.

"Says an 'angel' appeared
To her. Says God's Spirit knocked
Her up. Says we're 'favoured'!"

"You believe her?"

He nurses his ale and laughs.
"Would you? And you know what gets me?
Why didn't this 'angel' have the decency to
Have a word with me first? I'm the one's got
To raise it. I said to her, 'Go on then, what's
This angel look like?'"

"And?"

"Tall, fair hair, wings."
He shakes his head, drains his glass.
I sit in silence while he gets in the next
Round then ask: "What about her mum
And dad?"

He gives me a sideways glance
Like I'm mad. "You kidding? I'm the
One'll get it in the neck. You think
They'll believe she was 'covered
By the Holy Spirit'? What sort of mug's
Gonna buy that?"

Excuse me. What an insolent little poem.
You really are a shit, Stavrinides.

It's been said before.

Must you foul everything?
What's your point?

Just this. It's a preposterous
Bit of theological reverse engineering
By early Christians. "Our leader was

Executed, but he came back from
The dead in a giant 'fuck you'
To the Romans and Jewish
Establishment. Why? To save us.
From what?… Hell, and the
Punishment of the children of Adam.
How could a mere man do this?
Good point, no man could.
So… He must be God!
But Mary's his mother, Joseph's
His father. In that case… the Holy
Spirit must have been the father.
It 'covered' Mary."

So God committed adultery?

"No, it was a sinless and sexless
Conception between God
And a woman. Phew, got there
In the end!"

So now I have a question for you.
Is there nothing too ridiculous
For you to believe?

Termites

Try telling a colony of termites,
So vast in scale and industry,
It's city, a wonder of the world,
Engineered, ventilated, defended,
Its millions of lives weaving in
Intricate individuality a pattern
Fathomless and complex, its
Dramas and battles of life and
Death, its struggles for power,
Its organisation, social
Understandings, lives lived
In fierce determination, its
Successes and tragedies.
Try telling this colony it
Is utterly unimportant and its
Destruction will not trouble
The universe.

The Diamond

A salesman swaggers over to you
Hand outstretched, grinning,
"Look at this," he says, winking.
"You must buy it!" You look and
See what appears to be a diamond.
"It's perfect," he says. "You must
Buy it!" You aren't so sure so you
Ask to examine it. He shakes his
Head, juts his jaw, blinks and takes
A heavy breath through his nose.
"You don't trust me?" he asks,
And his hand goes to the pommel
Of his great sword. "You insult me.
It's lucky for you that I'll forgive the
Owner of this diamond." You ask
If there's a returns policy. He
Squints and spits at your feet.
"No returns!" he snarls.
You ask, *"If I examine it will it
Become less perfect in the process?"*
"No!" he shouts, looking to the heavens.
"Then why can't I examine it?"
He stares at you like you are scum
And unsheathes his sword.

What's the Point?

A mouse had jumped
Into an old trug in the
Garden, sheer-sided,
Half full of rainwater.
God knows its agony
Struggling for just a
Few more moments of
Wretched life before
Exhaustion saturated
Its lungs. And I thought,
As I looked at its floating
Little body, if all creation
Is about the human
Relationship with God,
And, even if it isn't, what's
The point? What's the
Point of that?

And I read in the paper
About a hedgehog
Shot at close range, left
Paralysed and suffering
Alone for days. "This poor

Girl must've been in so
Much pain," said the
RSPCA. "When she came
In to us she was dragging
Her hind legs behind her
And clearly had no use of
Them at all. There was
Nothing we could do for her.
She was suffering so much
The kindest thing was
To put her to sleep." And I
Thought, what's the point?
What's the point of that?

"The baboon eats the gazelle
Alive," says the voiceover.
The baby creature shrieks
With every bite, its entire belly
Ripped open, its leg nearly off.
I look away, appalled and
Disgusted with whatever power
Made this world. And I think,
How can it still be alive?
Each mouthful of living flesh
Torn from the body like leaves
From a tree and stuffed in

Casually. I feel cognitive
Dissonance seeing this and
Speaking of a "god of mercy".
Eating it alive! A tiny helpless
Thing, terrified, in agony,
Slowly dying. And I think
What's the point?
What's the point of that?

And I think, what's the
Point of this world at all?
Why make it first with
Dinosaurs for hundreds of
Millions of years, after billions of
Years floating around as
Dust, and rock? Those
Trillions of lives, both past
And living, entirely incidental
To our anthropocentric
Theologies. What's the point?
What's the point of that?

And our own kind, its different
Life spans, historical periods,
Education, circumstances;
If the test is belief, why not

Make the same conditions for all?
Even so, the test is not how kind
Or compassionate you are,
But the single choice of
What you are persuaded
To believe. And I cry,
What's the point?
What the fuck is the point of that?

politicians, clerics, moonshine
swindlers with something
to sell

if they promise you paradise
anticipate hell

specimen of vanity

when mankind dies or flies away
and the chimp or rat or whatever is
left by then is lord of earth, will god,
the infinite, fill a new vessel to die for
sins? the crucified chimp god?

if neanderthals had survived instead of
us would god be fully god, fully
neanderthal? is he hot-catting it
round the galaxy dying a thousand
different ways, the slut of self-sacrifice?

is only the intelligence of one species
ripe for such a union? are we so
different? or is the religion of the
slaughtered son the ultimate specimen
of our vanity?

Children of a Lesser God

"If There's A God He Will Have To Beg My Forgiveness"
                    Carved into the wall of a concentration camp cell

"In the concentration camp I had cried out in sorrow and in anger against God, and also against man, who seemed to have inherited only the cruelty of his creator"
                                                                    Elie Wiesel

"I form the light and create darkness: I make peace, and create evil: I the Lord do all these things."
                                                                    Isaiah 45:7

> maybe to create the best of all possible
> worlds you had to create the others
> too. each moment with its variants,
> stretching to infinity. but what do the
> inhabitants of all these refuse worlds
> make of their situations? how do their
> theologies make sense of what they
> cannot know: that they are the afterbirth
> of a greater perfection? look at this world's

religions and you have your answer.
i wonder too how anyone who is not a
child could contemplate for more than a
second and still insist *"this* is the best of
all that's possible."

but perhaps this world was created by
some lesser god, some saklas who
thought it looked easy and why not have
a go? "what's the worst that could happen?"
he winks and clicks his fingers.
we could tell him, couldn't we?
i wonder if our universe is hidden in some
cosmological sock drawer in the hope
no responsible deity will ever chance
upon it.

*"we're in here! come and find us! then beat
the little shit for all he's worth!"*

but deities stick together. it's always
been thus. and now the spokesmen for
the last few thousand years of psychosis
pipe up. *"how dare you speak of a demiurge?
our god is perfect."* the best of all possible gods?

well, put this in your pipe, anselm.
if i can imagine a better god than the one
who created this world then she must
exist. and, believe me, i can.

Come, Exterminating Angel

There is none that is good,
No, not one. The innocent
Young the selfish preamble
To what is to come.
That's where God went wrong:
Used water to cleanse
Instead of fire. Left a few
Seeds of the weed in the hope
They'd come up flowers.
The Devil is an innocent, I see
That now. "Pssst, over here!"
He calls the happy couple,
Brimming with useless tricks
To feed their appetites.
"Yeah?"
They scrunch hungrily as they look
The serpent over.
"What're you doing?" he gasps.
"What, these? They're delicious!
Try one."
"But you were forbidden! On pain
Of death!"

A smirk, a shrug. Adam holds
Her close from behind, pressing
Against her thighs. Whispers
In her ear. She doesn't even
Blush.
Too late, redundant, hacked
Away by Occam's Razor.
The poor old serpent can
Piss off back to the forest
To wait for chainsaws and
Bulldozers.

If Only You'd Run

If only you'd run.
But you were so green,
And the heart wants.

And who knows but
Maybe all roads lead
To different disappointments.

But if only you'd run!
Smiled politely and gone
On your way. I'd have

Fastened wings to your
Feet. Don't worry, I'd say,
I'll be fine, just fly, fly.

Just fly far until the sun
Bathes your face and
The sea calls your name.

Fly until the chains and
Disappointments slip from
You to the waters below.

Butcher's Hook

Is this what temptation is?
Hack your way to happiness
Through another's heart?
"Time will heal her wounds,
Then you'll both be happy."
Love, like art, is not kind.

Can I have it all?

Cupid smears bloody hands
Down his apron and sneers,
Reaches for his cleaver. And I
Understand love is a journey,
Two hearts sailing together
Under the same flag.

"You can do it," he says, tracing
A line to divide chambers and
Raising his massive hand in an
Arc above my aorta. "But the
Wounds'll be more severe than
Usual, and you'll never stop bleeding."

String Theory

They know, the scientists, the whole shebang is held
Together by duct tape and bits of string. Wasn't
That the real deal with Copernicus when he peered
Through his telescope at the cross-braced galaxy?
"You can't tell them that! They'd riot in the streets!"
They have their theory, how it all got going. The universe
Cranked into action, backfiring as it chugged down the
Road: uninsured, clutch screeching, puncture hissing
Slow but sure. "Who built this thing anyway? Can't
Someone *do* something?" But no one can. Jerry-built
On a wing and a prayer, it's a wonder it didn't conk out
In the middle of the highway long ago, other universes
Sweeping past majestic, horns blaring contempt.
And the human body, that "miracle of engineering"!
I'll hiss a secret in your ear: the miracle is this, that we
Get half way across a room without disintegration.
All those flaws and ailments and illnesses to fill
Libraries. Unsound spine, inflexible knee, narrow
Pelvis, meandering arteries, crowded teeth, backwards
Retina, mad gibbering monkey brain wired for war.

Entropy and strong force, like a couple of drunks slipping
On a mud patch, pulling a rope for all they're worth,
Though neither knows why. I'm yelling for entropy.
This game has gone on long enough. I'm bored and
Cold, and the referee's a wanker.

Stand Aside, Brutus! It's My Turn Now

We hate each other, Vovochka and I.
Just ask him. "Stavrinides? Who's
This Stavrinides I'm supposed to hate?"
"A free man, your excellency." His jowls
Set, nose wrinkles, and the smirk
Vanishes. He releases his oiled,
Muscular opponent reluctantly and
Takes the file. He prefers them
Domesticated, bred for docility, pliable,
Shall we say? "Why does he hate me?"
"Says you're a traitor to Russia,
A parasite ruining the world."

"I make Russia great again!" he thunders.
Russia's greatness is Russia's leader's
Greatness. It's all about you, isn't it,
Vovochka? Just another narcissistic
Dictator. And how do you achieve this
'Greatness'? By stealing their freedom!
Oh, when will serfs be done with tsars?
You rob the future of Russia's children

And call those who'd stop you traitors.

"Traitors always end in a bad way!"
Your words, Vovochka, your words.
"But I make Russia great!" So you keep
Saying. Let them eat cake, is that your
Argument? Tell us more about this
'Greatness'. Does it by any chance
Involve seizing the lands of others?
"The greatest geopolitical catastrophe
Of the twentieth century" – the collapse
Of the Soviet Union? That's your tragedy?
The end of the suppression of millions.
That's your tragedy?

What are you but the selection of a
Drunken old fool? What have you done
But kill a lot of people, enslave your
Country and loot the place? Putain is
Not Russia and Russia is not Putain.
You're nothing in yourself, not bright,
Not creative, not talented, just nothing,
Not even a decent human being.
What's your legacy but weapons and
Death? You fear for your reputation
And rightly so. You can't bully the unborn.

A poet has more power over the future
Than a tyrant. And I call upon it now,
As a lover of the land of Chekhov, Tolstoy,
Turgenev, Dostoyevsky and Pushkin,
As one who would give the Russian
People their longed-for freedom, I ask,
Who is the real friend of the Russians?

I call upon you. Let the name his parents
Gave him stand for all dictators, and
Let the seventh of October be celebrated
As a day to ridicule tyrants. Let those
Proud men, those strong men, be humiliated,
Imitated, scoffed at, scorned. Let comedians
Compete in mockery: "Where was Putain's
Dad on the night he was conceived? Out,
As usual, carousing with friends, leaving
Poor Mrs Putain alone, with only the dog for
Company…"

Let statues be erected of Anna Politkovskaya
And Boris Nemtsov shaking hands over your
Prone body, Anna's foot on your neck, Boris's
Foot bare in your face. May crowds gather in
Streets and burst into laughter when a speaker
Says your name. A hundred thousand people

All laughing at you. Let the seventh of October
Be a day for killing rats. A symbolic act. Let
Them joke it's not a good day to be vermin.
And you must have your statues too, Vovochka,
Skirted, in a nice blouse, wearing your dunce's
Hat. And someone will do it too. How can you stop
Them from your grave?

"Long live a free and proud Russia!" May the
Words of Boris Nemtsov adorn his bridge.
Russia's true son, fighting for liberty and
Justice. "But we *are* a democracy!" you
Snarl. Is that right? Where's the opposition?
Where there's freedom there's dissent always,
And lots of it. Human beings are disputatious.
Contrary, wilful, awkward. Dissenters are
The canaries of democracy, gauging the air
For that old poison power. The more
Concentrated the more deadly, dilution the
Only remedy. But then, you know all about
Poison, Vovochka, don't you?

Before You Give Power

Stick them in the middle of a field,
Switch on a hose to turn the soil
To glue. Hedge around with firethorn,
Razor wire, and sulphuric ditches.
Plant mines at random places inside
The field. Surround them with
Multitudes of guard towers full of
Crack shots with itchy fingers.
Fill the air with precision drones,
Motion-activated, primed for obliteration.
Then, and only then, most tentative
And provisional, give power.

In the Ranks of the Free Men

Look for me. You'll find me
In the ranks of the free men.
I take my stand as all men must
Who are men. I'll bare my breast
And offer my heart. I am nothing
But a flicker in the light that must
Burn forever. Against us the serried
Soldiers of the parasite kings:
The Putins, Erdogans, el-Sisis
And Maduros. We are men.
They are slaves and henchmen.
They march to quench our
Flame when they should kindle
Their own. Rise up! Rise up, you
Slaves and servants of the parasite
Kings! Give your children the gift
Of freedom. Put power in their hands
To choose stewards, muzzled as dogs
On a leash. Let them think as they
Will, speak as they will, do as they
Will, proud and free. And let the
Parasites who'd suck their marrow
Forever cringe at the coming
Vengeance of the man of liberty.